Mark M. Pomeroy, Henry Louis Stephens

Our Saturday Nights

Mark M. Pomeroy, Henry Louis Stephens

Our Saturday Nights

ISBN/EAN: 9783743301405

Manufactured in Europe, USA, Canada, Australia, Japa

Cover: Foto ©ninafisch / pixelio.de

Manufactured and distributed by brebook publishing software (www.brebook.com)

Mark M. Pomeroy, Henry Louis Stephens

Our Saturday Nights

OUR

SATURDAY NIGHTS

BY
MARK M. POMEROY,
AUTHOR OF "SENSE," AND "NONSENSE."

With Thirty Illustrations by H. L. Stephens.

NEW YORK:
Carleton, Publisher, Madison Square.
LONDON: S. LOW, SON, & CO.
MDCCCLXX.

Dedication.

TO THE

WIVES AND THE WORKING-MEN

OF THE WORLD,

This unpretending volume of Heart-written Chapters,

IS RESPECTFULLY DEDICATED,

WITH THE EARNEST PRAYER THAT IT MAY ADD TO

THE HAPPINESS OF

Hearts and Homes.

M. M. POMEROY.

NEW YORK, 1870.

CONTENTS.

	Page
I.—Sitting Side by Side	17
II.—Little Tin Pails	25
III.—Little Homes and Loved Ones	32
IV.—An Empty Hearse	40
V.—Home on a Shutter	50
VI.—Our Treasures	58
VII.—A Little Girl Whose Name is Lulu,	66
VIII.—Such a Little Coffin!	79
IX.—Kind Words from Woman's Lips	88
X.—Staggering Home	96
XI.—Worth of Woman's Love	105
XII.—Funeral Next Door	113
XIII.—"Only Two Laborers Killed!"	120
XIV.—Sinking to Rest	128
XV.—Standing before the Minister	136
XVI.—Burdens, and Those Who Bear Them,	144
XVII.—Rest for the Weary	155
XVIII.—Only a Poor Old Wood-sawyer!	163
XIX.—Home to the Loved Ones	172
XX.—About that Little "Yes"	180
XXI.—She Brought a Skeleton	187
XXII.—Going Home	196
XXIII.—Soliloquy of a Happy Man	203
XXIV.—Very Lonely	211
XXV.—About Our Neighbor	219
XXVI.—Plain Words to Those we Love	226
XXVII.—The Old Woman	237
XXVIII.—The Family Record	245
XXIX.—The Poor Old Man	255
XXX.—The Old Bureau Drawers	264

PROLOGUE.

TO-DAY an old friend came to our private room and asked:

"Did you know ——, of Milwaukee, when you lived there?"

"Yes."

"Did you know his daughter, who attended the —— Ward school?"

"Not the very pretty girl, who was so quick, attractive, and so full of promise?"

"The same."

"What of her? It is years since then — since we saw her in school one day, a little innocent girl, the pride of her parents, and the loved of all. What of her?"

"She is dead!"

"Well?"

"She died in this city this morning early. Poisoned herself last night. And the keeper of the house where she is says she must be taken away this afternoon, for a dead person in the house kills luck."

"Tell us more."

And he told us a heart-rending history. Years ago, nine as the calendar counts, the one who had tired of life, was a child in Milwaukee, a distant city of the West. She was quick, bright, attractive, and over-petted to her injury. Her temper was hot — her charms many. She lived for excitement. She went aside from the path her loved parents had so well walked, and loitered in the bowers of that incipient sporting life, where those enticed slyly taste the fruit, and inhale the perfume of attractive flowers growing so beautifully on deadly vines. The poison went to her brain; the early life became warped as present pleasures were planted for future pains.

She came and went; she roamed and romped like the butterfly that cares not for the winter; she sat, and rode, and walked, and talked, and rested with those who were feasting on her young loveliness, till home became irksome; and, when those who loved her best did kindly ask her of the present, she rebelled, and inhaled more of the poison, which drove the good from the heart.

She thought bowers were houses — rambles here and there amid vines and flowers were walks on the road to life.

And when the flower fell and the thorn pricked her soul, instead of returning to the true path and seeking only the love of one, she tried other labyrinths, and yet others. But, alas! the flowers fell everywhere, and everywhere the ugly thorns followed.

Then she left her home. Under a veil, and an assumed name she went to other cities: she came to this and drank deep of the poison which gave fewer and yet fewer hours of pleasure and more and more days of grief.

She was sought by this one — by that one. She gave to this one and to that one. Keeping nothing for herself, living only on the froth, and never drinking deeply of the pure water beneath. With her back upon hearts, home, happiness, and true manly friendship, she sought her home in the whirl, and lived to float, and drift, and be tossed from arm to arm, as whim, fancy, or devil-leading passion drew the ribbon, or shot glances from watching eyes that were but detectives for baser souls within.

. . . .

With our friend we went to her room. Up Broadway, and then into a side street. The ring of a door-bell brought a negro woman to open the walnut door of a palace, so-called. Up stairs to a beautifully furnished bedroom — three of us, besides the undertaker and his assistant, with a plain coffin.

Softly — in here. Ah! She will not waken. We looked, and the tears came into our eyes, for all she was but a dead unfortunate. She was once a girl — once a woman — once a loved child, beside whose little bed fond parents have stood and gazed on her sleeping beauty, and thanked God for her coming.

Finery everywhere. Silks, jewelry, articles of the toilet — pictures on the walls, dresses spotted by wine, books of prose and poetry.

A slipper on the right foot — silk stockings fitting her beautiful ankle — a little plain gold and three diamond rings on the fingers of the left hand, with a single-stone diamond-ring on the fore-finger of the right. A watch and chain lay noiseless on the bureau, stopped at fifteen minutes past four. Wonder if her life ran down then? God only knows! A little white kitten, with ribbon of blue about its neck, was sleeping on the pillow. Beside her was an empty ounce vial, which had contained laudanum.

She lay partly across the bed, one hand under her head, as if sleeping; her beautiful hair dishevelled, but such a sad, sick, desolate look on her face, the tears would not keep back.

She had died as she lived, in her finery. In her hand was a letter, — a good, kind, heart-written letter from one who had known her — who for years had tried to save her, for he loved her dearly. And the letter, with this chapter, we send to the writer, miles away, that he may know that the wayward, giddy, whirling, careless, beautiful, thoughtless girl he loved, for all she was not true to herself, was taken to a quiet grave by ones who have kind hearts, and who will never reveal his secret, for thus do those fraternally bound by each other.

She has gone, poor, heart-wrecked, desolatesouled, beautiful one. Let us hope to the care of those who will not pluck to destroy — who will fold her in loving embrace, and keep her with renewed purity for the one who so loved her, so kindly wrote to her, so well wished her, yet whose honest love and kind interest had so little weight with her here.

Her trunk was full of finery, and cards and pictures, and letters from the gay and thoughtless — full of odds and ends of a poisonous festival! And in a little box, as if sacred, the picture of father, mother, a sister, and two brothers. What shall we do with them? Send them home? They know not where she was, or is! They only know she is away, but under what name, what doing, alive or dead, they know not, for all they have often sought, as we know. Shall we tell them, or carry the secret with others and others we hold to the grave? What would our readers do? What would be *right?*

. . . .

A hearse and a carriage. At dusk, or nearly. Steadily we moved on down the street, meeting thousands. We put her in a plain coffin, for her life had been too plain of joy to mock her corpse and her great agony with a gilded casket. The beautiful one she had she despised — would not preserve — would not confide to the keeping of the one she loved and who loved her, so infatuated was she with the life she wanted to lead, so we would not insult her corpse with the hate of her life! She rested — but oh! that sad, heart-wrecked, pity-pleading face seeming to cry out from its perishing stillness:

"O God! O man! Give — give — give! Oh! give me back to that life, that love, that truth, that purity, that heart, — that *all* that would have been my salvation! O God! pity me, for the world does not! And give me *rest*, if I cannot have that hope, that faith, that bliss, that happy future I might have had but for careless wanderings."

Over the river we bore her away. We met others like her on the streets, little caring or dreaming who was in the hearse ahead, or the carriage following. We took her away, as they will be taken.

If the graves of the lost ones could cry out, who could listen to the terrible wail? The love and passion-songs of earth — the discordant unisons of perdition, sufficient of themselves to curse millions and hold their souls down to agony. Oh! the present — the future! The minute — the Eternity! O Father in Heaven! give us all will and power to save, but no heart to wreck, to destroy!

We buried her as the sun went down on this beautiful Saturday Night. And we rode slowly home as the hearse went its way for another, or to wait an order!

And we looked out of the carriage window as the dead one can look out of the window of the past to see where she mistook the road! And we saw people hastening to and fro — this way and that, eager to reach home. Poor girl — she was eager to reach home! So she went uninvited — glad to rest in the grave, *anywhere*, rather than in her wild, heart-rending, soul-harrowing thoughts.

Well — she is gone. God be kinder to her *there*, than she was to herself here! Fearful was the load she took with her! Every flower a thorn — every ramble a walk with fiends — every reckless dalliance a garment of torture woven on earth with the bright side out, to be worn there, with the stings piercing the soul.

And God pity her parents — and him who loved her. She is at rest: the waters of the river, and the rack of the torture that drove her to death may purify her — we hope they will.

To-night we are going on a visit. To the bedside of our friends. We will kiss them while they sleep, and they will not know we were there. We will straighten the coverlets over the hearts and to the throats of those we love — will kiss them again and pray God to keep them all in the right path. And we will go for hours before we sleep, to the bedsides of those miles and miles away, and see which are to be lost or to be saved — to the bedsides of those who sleep in sin and reckless, *unloving* passion, and kiss them once never so softly for the mothers and fathers who have lost them forever.

Then to the sleeping forms of those who have lost loved ones in the terrible whirl, and whisper of the meeting Over There, where the truants will return, and then in the cribs, cradles, and beds of those who have good fathers and mothers to watch over them, and will with the loving and the living look with joy and pride on the sleeping ones, who little know in their childish dreams that while they sleep, while all is still, warm hearts are beating and tear-glistening eyes are looking and praying that they may live for those who most truly love them — from God to man, and not be taken to the grave as was the poor, storm-tossed, heart-wrecked, beautiful child of misfortune we in sadness helped bury this Saturday Night.

INTRODUCTION.

THIS is Saturday Night.

With others, in general, the labor of the week is ended. All over the land are weary men, and weary women and dear children who have homes, and dear ones who have none.

"Well, what of them?"

Only this: they need more true, earnest friends than they have; they are the toiling ones, who deserve kind words, and who should, who will, be kinder to each other.

Long years have we suffered and battled for ideas, principles, and rights. By this ordeal we have learned to think. And to think of others. Of working-men, all over the land. Of weary, worthy, patient wives. Of children; of the good and the bad, everywhere. Now, as GOD is our judge, we do feel kindly to all men; we feel more than a deep, truthful, earnest, enduring interest in those who would be happy; who would live to a purpose, who would have homes here on earth, and glorious happiness in the beautiful Land of the Leal where we hope to rest some day forever.

Saturday Night! and others are at rest. Perhaps in the hours this night before the old week dies, we can write something which will make men and women happier, and homes happier, and loves stronger, and children stronger to live for a great and good purpose. Would to that GREAT FATHER we are not one bit afraid to meet, and who has given us such a full faith for a happy and useful future, we could talk as one would sit of an evening and converse by his fireside with friends dearly loved, and in whom real interest is felt, — to all the wives, the children, the working-men of the land.

But this we cannot do.

And so, faithful pen, with which we have written more than a thousand of columns, and millions of words, will you aid us in a little work each Saturday Night? They tell us you are mightier than the sword; and we believe it. Therefore we choose you as our friend, and enlist you in the work of labor while others rest. And so sit we down to our labor. With a heart warm and full of love to those who really wish to be good, and true, and loving, and happy, we hold thee Heavenward, that the sunbeams of earnest interest from the beautiful spirit Home may rest on thy diamond point, and that good influences may be in our heart direct from those with whom we hold such sweet communion, that the words we write on the coffin-lid of the dying week may make better those to whom this heart-written volume is dedicated.

And do not, good home ones who sit by hearth and fender; who know the depth and purity of earnest love; who with us are often weary, think ill of us for this plain, homely writing. We would not dictate, nor compel you to think with us. But we would see you all happier, and deem it no wrong nor cause for shame to sit down while others rest, to write from the heart of an earnest man, who has known grief, sorrow, labor, struggle, privations, and success, kind words to all, and especially to the ones to whom this volume is dedicated for reading on all the morrows, as we begin this our earnest home-work Saturday Night.

Thine for the Right,

M. M. POMEROY.

SITTING SIDE BY SIDE.

THE *Rain! the Rain!*

How it patters on the panes, runs down in rivulets, as if the windows were sorry and in tears! Our work for the week is well-nigh finished—perhaps the work of our life will be finished this Saturday Night.

It will be for many; and the tears of sorrow

for the loved ones will patter like rain-drops on strained and grief-crimsoned hearts.

How the old memories are recalled by incidents! Near a score of years ago! How time comes and is lost in the mist of the past! In a room not so large nor so nicely furnished as this. No gas-burners holding back the curtains of darkness, but a simple lamp.

It was Saturday Night.

She sat right there—on a little ottoman. We sat right here, as it seems. Never a picture so distinct. It rained; and the drops danced and spattered as they were storm-whirled against the panes in that blessed country home. She sat there, we here. It was not far from here to there, nor does it seem an hour since thus we sat. And yet it must be. Men cannot suffer so much in an hour!

She was beautiful. Her eyes were unlike any others we ever saw. She talked with them, and every word was in spirit-melody, "*I love you, darling.*" Do you wonder memory is faithful?

Her hands were in ours. They were such soft, white little hands, who could help kissing them? We thought them the most beautiful in the world. And her eyes—they talked to us so eloquently! And her lips—none like them in all God's creation. Purity, fervor, love, sweetness, devotion, confidence. Earnest trusting and quiet heart-rest—these were the unwritten volumes her lips told as we read, from their red readiness, while the rain pattered much as now. Years, years, years; but still that night!

We sat and talked as others have and as others will. The sky was cloud-covered, but not our hearts. It was very, very dark without, and the storm howled as if in envious anger at the picture within, and spent its spattering venom on rill-coursed panes in vain. What we talked of, or how long, we cannot tell—yet we can. It was of the past which seemed so short—the present which was so bright for all the darkness outside —the long-coming future across the broad waves of which we launched many little boats, and were very happy to see them sailing away to distant isles we had been told were 'way out in the ocean of the future, and to be found by somebody! The isles existed only in *that* direction, yet some folks send their ships in all directions! And the farther they sail the further therefrom. Alas! there are many ships idly cruising, wrongly mated, never nearing the beautiful groves of the sea, but at last sinking from sight while the waves roll on, and other boats or ships sail over that spot perhaps to sink just beyond!

But we thought of these things while the rain pattered and the wind in gustful fever raged without. So close she was to us. Yes—hand and heart—lip and life.

"How the wind blows and the trees wail! Is it not a fearful night?"

"Yes: are you not afraid?"

"Afraid? No, darling; for you are here."

She wore no diamonds, nor was her garb of silk. We had no houses, lands, or wealth, but never was boy or man so rich. Her eyes seemed like portals of Heaven, from which came most wondrous light of love, and not gentler ever was nod of beautiful flower than the silent, soul-sealing kiss on forehead then so gently given.

No matter how wild the storm, how dark the night. Hearts that are truly heart-warmed never feel the outside cold or pang of poverty.

. . It is late. The storm is over. My darling must rest. As the storm has gone, and the stars are coming, so will troubles go and joys come if we but live for the within, but not in selfishness.

Closer and still closer. Yes, very soon will we come. And, now, darling, this kiss,—

> "Good-night, loved one, *good-night!*
> But ere from thee we part,
> Take this one kiss of love — *good-night!*
> It tells how dear thou art."

The morrow came. . . . They found her *asleep!* The little hand was on the pillow; the once red, now pale cheek rested on her hand; the lips parted as if to smile. So they found her when came the morrow; so they told us. But she slept in a little narrow coffin. The physician said she passed away instantly, from over excitement of the heart.

> "Good-night, loved one, *good-night!*
> But ere from thee we part,
> Take this *last kiss* on earth — *good-night!*
> It tells how dear thou art."

. . . .

Many the Saturday Night have we sat by a little grave looking into the eyes which live forever. And she ever seems to us as then, and we even say,—

"*Yes, very soon we will come!*"

And when the wild wind roars and the storm-fiends hold revels in air; when the great drops patter on leaf and rock; when the trees in the forest near by bend in terror, toss their limbs, and seek to prostrate themselves before the Power of the elements; when others sit by little fires or side by side, we love to sit there by that hallowed spot, and talk with her as of yore. She is not dead. Ah, no! She was too young—she is at school with God, waiting our coming. And for years we have been ready, and mayhap we can *go home* some Saturday Night like this. We know she is waiting and wondering why we do not come; and that she will wait till we come, and then will have been found that beautiful isle we missed on the ocean, or rather which we did not start from shore in search of, for our pilot was taken.

. . . .

Sometimes the clouds gather very, very dark over our life, and we go away—no one knows where. And we sit beside that little grave, hold her hand in ours, look into her eyes, and launch our little ships as we did years ago. And the memory of then—the hope of *then* makes us brave and stout of heart. And we try to be good, for she was good, and to live so that when we cross the ocean of sleep between us, and step to meet her coming, she may not be ashamed of us.

When the work comes for us to do, we do it, just as we told her we would. That Saturday Night we were very poor in all save hope and pluck, and it is hard to lift sympathy away from such as the good, the loved, and the trusting as that night sat with us while the rain beat as when we began this chapter. These rain-storms are stepping-stones to the hallowed past, and they are laden with the resolves and promises made that night before the Great Eternal. And but for others we would wish that there would come a beating rain and a storm on whose wings we could ride to meet her, and in honor of whose memory we write a little chapter under her angel influence each Saturday Night.

II.

Little Tin Pails.

GOD bless the little tin pails!

To-night we saw them going home, — a thousand and more of them. They were carried by men who toil — by the workingmen, who are sneered at, and snubbed, and jostled against, and pushed aside by the gilt-edge fashionables whose hands are soft and whose hearts are hard. The little tin pails went out this morning, and they went in to-night. The man who had one in his hand swinging by his side, was weary and foot-sore, just as we have been a thousand times, and no one to pity us, save the one who waited our coming, and the God who has pity for all who need.

We saw the laborers go by this morning, their little pails full, their step quick and elastic; for it will not do for laboring men to be late! The rich, who carry furs and gold-clasp purses, and who pet their poodles, may be late or not go at all; but the honest man, with hard palms and an uncertain future—he must be on time. 'Way up stairs, down cellar; in the close, sticky, ropy, thickened air of the tenement house, where humanity is huddled like sheep, their little pails were filled. A wife arose while her tired husband was sleeping "just a moment more," and with silent step walked the floor till the scanty meal of the morning was ready. Then she called him, and the tired man arose, wishing he did not have to go forth thus early. And while he ate hurriedly, the hand he once so loved to kiss filled that little pail. A slice or two of bread, a little cold meat, some salt and mustard, and perhaps a piece of pie or cake; mayhap an egg, or cold potatoe; and perchance, in a little cup on top the pail, a pint of coffee. Then the knife and the spoon were slipped in, and he hurried away.

Work, work, work! hour after hour. Thinking of this and that; of the past, of to-day, of to-morrow. Hammer, saw, pound, brush, stitch, file, drill, shovel, lift, watch, strain muscle and strain mind. Hours go by—noon comes. The little pail is welcome treasure. It comes at hour of rest, with its fill of food. The tired man eats, and he thinks of home and the loving hands that filled his little pail, and his heart grows strong; and when the noon hour is over, he works and works, and he works for her and for them, and for a better home, and a time when to rest a day is not to rob the loved ones.

And he looks back over the years to the time when he wondered if she loved him, and to the Saturday Nights when he hurried home, and washed his face, and his hands, his neck, his body; when he put on his best, and no matter how tired, hastened to meet her, to see her, to put his hand in hers, to take one, two, three,— a score of kisses from the lips so loved, and to look, oh! so far down into the depths of the eyes which were his choicest mirrors. She was young then. Now she is old or growing old. He works in the shop. She toils in the house, and, perhaps, goes out to labor, to help him earn a home.

Monday — Tuesday — Wednesday — Thursday — Friday — Saturday! Six days of toil, of waiting, of working, of hoping, of doubting, of hard labor for the loved ones, and the life all prize. The little pails go and come, day after day, till they build houses, stores, churches, towns, cities, countries! And they last often after those who carry them have gone home to the land of the leal, and the rest that knows no more disturbing. Up in shops, 'way up stairs and down cellars, on the streets, along the wharves, here, there, everywhere, they go and come, till they have worn out the laborer and enriched the employer.

And the men who carry them, and all who toil, are the ones who build the country and finish the town. The miser looks at his gold or his bonds; the bondholder rides in his carriage, quaffs his wine, lolls back on his sofa, sports his jewelry, counts his bonds, figures on his income, pays no taxes, and lives like a lord. He builds no houses. He erects no stores. He piles not one brick above another till a beautiful improvement be made; but he robs the little tin pail of all it earns, and empties the sweat it holds Saturday Night into the crucible of Congressional protection, then pours out perfumery for himself and his loved ones, who are mincy, and nobby, and stylish, and soft of palm; who wear silks, and catch their skirts in hand as they pass the little tin pail lest the robe of aristocracy be touched with honest spots. We do not like the mincing worshippers of poodles, and the ones who sneer at the laborer and rob him of his earnings.

For an hour we have seen them go by. Little tin pails, more precious and worthy than diamond necklaces. The ones who carry them seem tired, as we are tired from over-writing. God guide those who carry them to happy homes, and give the weary man a night of rest. And to him we say, God knowing we mean but good,—

"Go home and rest. Hang the pail on its nail or stand it upon its shelf. Then draw off your boots, if the chores be done. Kiss your wife as you did years ago, when, on a Saturday Night, you told her you loved her so dearly. Call back the love-light. Be good and kind to her. Rest her palm in yours. Smooth back the hair from her brow, and hold her cheek to your neck as in days of the past. She has worked all the week, in her room — busy, busy, ever busy, for woman's work is never done. She has not had the company you have. She has counted the hours, waiting your coming, for the home of the poor is sometimes lonely. Be kind to her, love her, talk to her, read to her. Read this chapter to her, and tell her you are trying to make your home and your loved ones happy. Save your money. Beautify your home, be it never so humble. Do not squander it for rum or in dissipation, to weaken your strength, shorten your days, and embitter the final hour. And try, working-man and brother, how much you can do to make home happier, and our work will be to help you."

III.

LITTLE HOMES AND LOVED ONES.

LIKE the stars of God, they are scattered all over the land. Little homes and loved ones, where men and women and children are far happier than they think for! To-night marks another Saturday Night fold in our record — one more shortening of the programme of life. All the week we have worked till both brain and body are tired, weary, and rest-needing. All the week in the great city—hard walls, with their glass eyes on either side of us—hard floors to the city under feet—hard hearts and selfish ones sifted in with the mellow and liberal ones, till never was there a more wonderful kaleidoscope than that of life in this wrestling-ground for those who struggle to please the beggar of Mammon.

Rich and poor all about us. And which are the happier? God knows! We know the brown stone fronts, the marble fronts, the expensive palaces, are all well enough; but they are filled with more furniture than happiness. Dollars bring care and old age to the heart. They lead into dissipation, into recklessness, into living for those who pass by to envy rather than for those who kiss a fond good night!

Shoddy and aristocracy, selfishness and snobbishness, ignorance and duplicity, extravagance and unhappiness, make the set, and tiresome is the dancing when people live for their eyes and the eyes of others rather than for their own hearts.

The happy homes and the humble ones. The little homes and the loved ones. Where labor has a friend, honesty an advocate, love a votary, and life a noble purpose, there you will find happiness. The rich yawn, and gape, and drink wine, and grow weak, thin of blood, and lean in relish; they follow fashion to the emasculation of vigor and zest for the enjoyable that springs from love; they sit at the card-table, dress for the opera, dream of stylish sensations, grow life-languid, pause and sigh for the lusty, vigorous manhood and happiness that homes with the laboring and the loving.

The poor envy the rich their fine clothes, fine houses, handsome carriages, wealth of jewelry, and life of ease. But the rich are the most envious. A thousand times have we heard them sigh for the health and brain-rest of the man who labors to support his loved ones. The contents of our hearts, not of our safes, make us rich!

"How much did he leave?" asked a man, when the millionaire died. "Half a million," said one. "A million," said another. "Two million in bonds," said the third. "*I know!*" spake a laboring man, as he sat on his work-bench, eating his noon-time lunch from a little *tin pail*. "How much?" asked they all. "How much did he leave when he died?— *all he had!*"

And the mourners returned from the tomb, drying their eyes by the way. And they went to their lawyers for consolation, and retorted the memory of the dead man till they extracted the last grain of gold, hated each other, and cursed him forever that he *left them* no more!

That was his wealth; that was what he worked for to put in the coffin with him. The petted calf was fatted and died for the benefit of the feasters — the *worms!*

That was their rich man. Ours is another man. "Who?" We will tell you before the Saturday Night be gone. He is a workingman. He is a laborer, with look of health, hard of palm, but mellow of heart. He works in a shop or an office. He lives to live and make others happy. He goes and comes at stated hours. He leaves the echo of a hundred kindnesses in his home as he goes forth to his labor. He leaves a kiss on the lips of his little ones to keep them warm, and on the lips of his wife to make her heart light and keep her from saying cross words; he takes a kiss as he goes, and all the hours of toil thinks of and works for the dear ones of the little home and the loved one.

All the day he pounds, or files, or saws,

or sets type, or feeds a press, or strikes in the forest, or in the mines, finding gold for the bondholders; or labors, as others labor, for the welfare of the loved ones and the making of their homes more beautiful. He is good, and true, and brave, and earnest; sober, careful, kind of heart, and loved, oh! so dearly, by the one who tremblingly said "Yes," to his asking once, the time now agone. *He is our* rich man. He works and he sings, he toils and he whistles, he labors and he saves to make home happy and add to the comforts of his little retreat. And the wages are a rich reward that labor brings, for its honesty is its wealth. And his home grows in beauty as he nears the grave, and his loved ones follow him on his journey to that land where angels are our guides, and stars the lights of God's eternal illumination!

This week a book; next week a picture of some beauteous scene, or of some man who has won a place in the hearts of the good; and next week a newspaper or magazine to interest each week. Then a carpet, a curtain, an easy-chair, a mirror, a flower-plot, another picture — home beauties and comforts rather than the heavy eyes, bloated faces, and rotting manhood of those who go, even in their own advance, to ruin by the torturing paths of dissipation.

Wife, have you a husband like our rich man? Then love him. Forgive him when he stumbles, help him up when he falls; throw your arms about him, aid him, care for him, cheer him, encourage him in the good, and be happy, no matter if your home be a little one. We are all happier than we think we are. We are all happier than others!

There are working-men who hate us, who know us not, who do not know how earnestly we think and strive to benefit them, no matter how we differ politically. We would see them happy, their homes beautiful, their earnings saved by themselves; and to all these men, true kings of nobility, we wish prosperity and happiness, and loved homes to call their own each and every Saturday Night.

IV.

An Empty Hearse.

IT went by not five minutes since. A black, cold-looking lonesome hearse, drawn by two sorry-looking horses, followed by two old-looking carriages, as it returned from the City of the Dead over yonder. The rain fell in a sort of drizzle, cold and sickening, as the driver, wrapped in an old waterproof, bent his face to the storm and urged his team to a little faster trot, as if anxious to get futher from the grave and to hasten home to rest with his loved ones. And the mourners were anxious to keep up, and their steaming horses did.

As the hearse passed, we saw by the rollers on its floor—they were far apart—that a large coffin had rested thereon; and in the sanctum, when it was reached, we stopped writing to think. And in this wise ran our thoughts:

That driver must have a singular life. Every day going with his peculiar freight, each day the better learning the road to the spot he will in time reach, as well as any of his customers, no matter whether he ever saw the final city or the road leading thereto! Wonder if he ever counts his trips as he sits on his box waiting, and wondering what number his last will be,—the trip but one way for him, two ways for the rest?

And is it not a singular journey when a man must go alone? No guide! No friend along to help kill time, for time has helped kill him. No asking how far to this station or that; in fact, no *starting* on the trip till hours after you have reached your final destination!

Who was it? We do not know. Millions do not know. Millions do not care,—do not even care to care! The empty hearse dodges up Broadway, of less account than a milk-cart. Somebody has *gone home* this Saturday Night, and the great world cares no more for the sorrow which rests in the home once his than for the breeze which passed yesterday. But there is a vacant spot in his home—a wound so deep in some heart or hearts, surely God must pity and heal! No matter how poor he was, somebody loved him. Perhaps he was sinful,—we all are,—yet somebody loved him and looked for his coming; and when the last look came, and the unspoken words died out as he died, and the last pressure of his hand, hard though the palm might have been, was felt; and when his soul cut loose from earthly moorings to soar away to the infinite, then went the hot leaden plummet of sorrow, oh! so deep into some heart, which may God pity.

. . . .

This *death* is a terrible thing to us; not because it is death, but because it is the parting with life and from those who have grown into and all around our hearts as sunshine plays through branches and rests on flowers. For the future we have no fears. God is mercy and mercy is God. God is the concentration of Faith; and those who rest on Him and His promises never will fall or sink. The future is all of joy to us—all of life, love, goodness, usefulness, and higher intellect, with greater responsibilities and capacities for enjoyment and none for sorrow. It is not death, but the parting with life and loved ones for a time, that bothers and sets thought in a quiver.

To die and be forgotten is something—yet it is nothing, for those who forget us will be nothing to us *over there!* To die and bid farewell to earth will be but ceasing to look upon a miserable sketch and feasting our eyes upon a more beautiful picture than man ever saw; to come like a bit of sunshine upon those who have gone before us to look upon it, and to be gladdened, when those who sincerely mourn come to tap us on the shoulder as we are gazing on the beautiful, saying to us, with golden smiles and love-lit eyes: "*Darling,* I have come!"

But it is terrible to die and know that you are dying. The loved one or ones go and come. The room becomes tiresome. The couch has no rest in it. The familiar walls seem as if already in the possession of another. Some loved one comes with drink or food to

An Empty Hearse.

sustain life; she pushes back the hair from an aching brow; she moves like an angel, with light, careful step, for her shoes are of love; and she touches *so* gently, and her pure lips touch your hand or face with their wondrous electricity; her eye is, oh! so sad and tearful, as she waits like one in treble agony for that robber whose approach she fears, for he will take "all the world" from her.

And to leave her!—that is the agony! Who will care for *her* as the one who is dying? Another will in time, perhaps, and perhaps not; after the birds have twice twittered their vernal odes,—after the flowers have twice listened thereto,—some one else will be dear as you have been, and kiss the lips you would not now have him kiss for all the world—for they are *hers!* Another hand will hold hers Saturday Night—or hold his; another eye will call the love flames to hers; another breast will be the pillow on which your loved one has so often rested; another arm will hold to the heart the dear one you cannot bear to part with. And then all the little keepsakes you prize will be emptied into some old box or into the fire, and she will find no joy in the little things which once were so prized by both as dottings left by happy passing hours.

And this is agony to those who love. And it is agony to think that, perhaps, no one else will care for your loved ones as you did, and that they may suffer some day. Then, weary one, how much fuller the cup of love she will bring with her sunshine when she comes to surprise, as you wait to welcome in the beautiful land of the leal!

. . . .

Before long the carriage of dignity will call for us — for writer and reader. Not this Saturday Night, but before some of the next ones. And who will miss us? Who of all

An Empty Hearse. 47

the world will be sorry? We know; and because we know we shall be missed, we care not to die just yet. But some day the hearse will call for us; the long box will be shoved into it; we shall be taken to the silent city, and in time forgotten unless we work well and leave good deeds to call us to mind.

Their tears will fall, and we know it. Not mock tears, but real ones, bursting up from the heart, for a friend will have gone. And then somebody will hold up our garments, look at them, and give them away. Somebody will look at the watch we carry, and say, " 'Twas his." And somebody will wear at parties the little cross we wear, emblem of our faith, and forget, perhaps, that its purity is not its only worth.

And somebody will claim and have the thousands of beautiful presents, keepsakes, mementoes, and purchases of our sanctums, but will any one prize them as we do? And men of law, executors, and administrators, will open drawers, safes, desks, and read hundreds of letters and documents, finding in them nothing of value, as they think, all the while wondering what we kept them for. And they will find political records, reputations of friends and enemies, letters and documents in cypher, deeds and titles to property, unpublished chapters of life, foolish letters and good ones, scraps, trinkets, etc., no one can tell the use of. And they will find scores of packages of letters marked, "Private — to be burnt, unopened, by a friend when I am dead." Will they heed our request? Yes — if they are friends. And all the little things, trifles in themselves, but volumes each, will be tossed aside. Little buttons, bows, ties, pieces of ribbon, shells — hundreds of precious things to us, will be thrown away; for those who know not their history know not their worth to us, as stepping-stones, when, after all our work is done, each day we walk in fancy back the river of time to the days of long agone.

· · · · · · · ·

Well, it is well we can not all live forever; there would be no more good folks up yonder, nor bad ones down there. This would be a tiresome world if eternity was life here! Thank God, there is a home over the river — an end to this work which wears us out — a time to quit — a hope for the future, and a land where we shall meet the loved ones, the dear ones, the worshipped ones who have been called to their rest before us. And thank God that while we live, all of us can make others happy if we will; we can fit ourselves for happiness hereafter, can mellow the mould in which we must rest, by being truer, nobler, and better than we would be but for those we love and who love us and our coming each Saturday Night.

.V.

HOME ON A SHUTTER.

IT was a very cold Saturday Night, only a few days ago. The wind howled like some watch-dog from the infernal, hunting for one absent. Signs creaked as they swung, and rich men on the street hurried by with fur-wrapped ears and well-gloved hands.

All the week gone but this. An hour more

labor and we will close the business desk, and finish the week with a Saturday Night article. First, we must make a call six blocks away.

Out in the cold. How the air dances in to warm by our body as we walk along. Five o'clock and thirty minutes by the great clock up there over the City Hall: later than we thought, so we hurry across Chatham and up Centre.

From a cross street they come, four men, stout, rough-clad, hard-palmed, honest-hearted men, with regular step and sad faces — four working-men, to us unknown.

Four men carrying a shutter from some window. And on it is a man, dead,— one hand under his head, as if he slept. He sleeps, and he sleeps well! Over his face is thrown a well-worn coat he used to wear. It does not keep him warm, but it keeps the wind from driving the hair into a horrid wound over his temple, from which blood and brains ooze slowly, as if sorry to leave their home!

"Who is he?"

"Michael O'Brien, sir. He was just killed, sir."

"How, and where!"

"He was working with us, sir, down on Pearl Street, on a new building, when a capstone gave way, sir, and took poor Michael in its fall; and never a word spoke he since. And we are takin' him home to his wife and children, and it's a sorry night they'll have of it, for they loved him so!"

And with the four went another to lend a hand to those in need. Went to a workingman's home on another street. Into the door, up two flights, slowly — slowly, for the stairway is very narrow.

"What is the matter?"

"Open the door wider, for it is all sorrow we bring. Steady, men — on that chair — on this — softly, now. There, now, we are home with him, and God pity those who mourn! Words are of no use here. Even curses would not be heard. Tear off the coat — kiss the lips — kiss them again and again; lift your head and look into that face, upon that wound; press back the hair from the brow you have so often kissed. Stand back, men — stand back! *She* is the one that needs pity, for hers is the heart that now drinks in sorrow as never before.

Good-night, friends; we will go now. Never mind thanks; never mind who we are, — simply a man who came to aid, not to gratify curiosity.

Down stairs and into the street. Sobs and wailing behind us. Her voice, and the voice of two little ones, now fatherless, and face to face with death. God pity them. . . . .

The table was ready to spread. The room was being put in order against *his* coming, but not in this way. The work of the week nearly ended; waiting for him and his smile, his greeting, his coming with his earnings,— a little present for each of the little ones, and a warm, rich, honest love-kiss for the one who is now leagues away in the terrible valley, heart-broken and in agony.

All the week he toiled, as we learned, early and late. A strong, honest, healthy man, working to better his home and make his loved ones happy. His hands were hard, but he was good. He was unused to sharp tricks, to speculations, to legalized robbing; he was simply a working-man, and his loss is not felt! Not felt! God above us! The capstone that fell and crushed his life was a million times lighter than the loss she bears or the sorrow she knows!

He was but a laborer. He toiled all day. He earned of dollars but few, but he earned them, and that is better than to steal them. He was but one man among many, but he was a man, a husband, a father. He lived in no palace, but he had a happier home to go to nights than many a man of wealth. Hour after hour he worked. Stone after stone he hauled up. His mark was left on many a spot where men of labor leave their marks. But now he has gone.

No band will follow him to the grave; no long line of empty carriages filled with men chatting of horses, of bonds, of houses, of wine, of women, of nothing, will follow him *home* but loving hearts will mourn for him, for he deserves tears.

Fold and put away his clothes. Put back that plate; leave back the knife, fork, and spoon; no more set his chair to the table, for he has gone home where there are no Saturday Nights terrible as this is to the mourners. Then, weeping one, live with his memory. Life is an enigma. Death is the reality. We meet here, we become acquainted, and then the one most loving goes to make a home over there.

Think of his kind words, his good acts; think of the good he did while he lived; forget the hasty words, the unkind ones, if ever he spoke them. And you who have to-night the forms of loved ones in your homes waiting for the tomb, God pity you. And you who do not have death with you to-night, may you not have it for years to come. Welcome the tired ones as they come from the shop. Give them a kiss and a kind word. Make home pleasant, and call to its sacred reach the loved ones. Let those who labor make their homes happy, and their home ones happy; and, when our work be done here, may all who are deserving live in memory loved, as was poor Michael O'Brien.

Who of the rich ever think of the poor? Who of them will remember kindly, and give good thoughts to the ones who toil? They have hearts and loves, as have the rich, and quite often better ones. They have wives, and little ones, and aims, and desires. They are deserving, as all are who labor. They make the city and finish nature. Yet few there are who care for the working-men, the ones who live in tenement houses. If the rich would treat those who labor better, the world would be the gainer, and therefore do we ask those who are favored by fortune and unjust laws, when they go home, to give a thought to the poor ones, the weeping and heart-broken ones, who are always with us, and oftener more deserving than those who pass them by with a sneer from Monday morn till Saturday Night

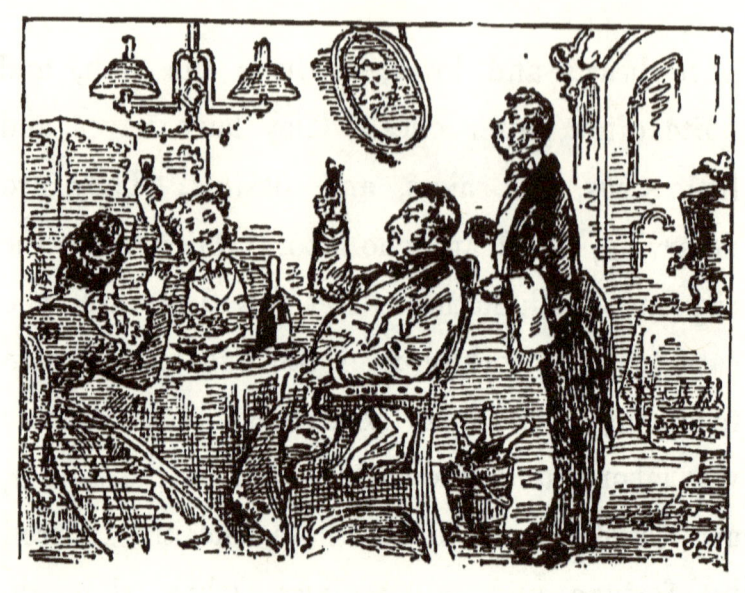

VI.

Our Treasures.

WEALTH!

Before the sun went home this Saturday Night to tell God who had striven the hardest for heaven the week past, a millionaire rode by. He lives in a palace — we in a cottage. He has his coachman, outriders, servants, and waiters; we have not one.

He hoards dollars as we do the kind words of our friends, while his bonds are many, as are the curses we could heap upon those who, by legislation, made him rich and our friends poor. He is a millionaire; we are not. He lives at ease; we live by labor.

He dines at six. Silver and gold are upon his table. A professional cook tempts his wine-wet palate with viands none but the rich can buy. Servants, with sharp eyes to detect the slightest wish, hasten to hand him this and that. His wife sparkles the diamonds which robbed her eyes of love's wondrous lustre when she took them as the price of her heart! Jewelry, lace, silk, satin, plush, velvet, damask, silverware, gas-light mellowed by tinted shades of glass or porcelain, broadcloth and echoes of dissipation, —grand, costly, and envied in *his* home. He eats and he drinks. He dines and he wines. He rides and he thrives. Servants open doors, brush the lint from lappel and body, the dust from hat and boot. He gives checks and lives high, does the millionaire. And his children are cared for by professional nurses. They call him governor. His wife, by forms ceremonial, empties the purse he fills, and is happy in her rouge, her diamonds, her carriage, her toilet, her establishment, her position in that society which is kept within proper "bonds."

"Happy?"

No, she is not happy! Wives by marriage and wives by brevet! He lives here; he revels there, where wine and dissipation pave the way for further chapters but nearer home. He rode by in his carriage, and a thousand turn to mention and envy him whose home is rich, but far from heart-warmed. Yes, envy the millionare. And you may, but the glitter of his coach, the style of his carriage, the prancing of his horses, the sparkle of his diamond-covered wife, the rich odor of his anticipated dinner, have no charms for us, and we envy him not.

. . . .

WEALTH!

Yes, we are rich. Ours is a cottage, or a cabin, if you will. It is up-stairs — on the ground floor — in the city — in the country — of wood — of stone — of brick. Marble for the rich — brick for the poor! We have no carriage, no horses, no servants, no wine, no haughty or petulent keeper of the purse to purchase from with gifts when love hungers for the beautiful fulfilment! But we have a *home*. The rooms are not large. The furniture is not rich; but in that home is a greater treasure than the millionaire ever possessed. *Our* Treasure. Our *Darling*. Sworn to love. Bond paying golden interest hourly. Dearer treasure than money ever purchased. *Our Darling!* Pretty soon we shall put the pen in its place and go and meet her. Shall walk, for we have no carriage. And shall walk fast. And we shall meet her at the door, and bless God for the kiss of welcome. And as we walk side by side to the chair set for us, can draw our treasure to our heart, and say, "I love you, darling." And she welcomes us Saturday Night, and every night; and her pure, true, trusting, and beautiful love keeps us from wandering. And we sit by our little fire, hand in hand. Diamonds never threw light as do the eyes of our darling, for they light from soul to soul, making noonday of otherwise night. And she gives us, oh! such tempting welcome. No servants are near to listen and tell. The rattle of playthings on the floor disturbs us not, for we knew it, and 'twas as God intended. And as no one hears, we sit, palm to palm, and thus come the words of the heart:—

"Darling, *I love you!* All the day have I toiled, till hand and brain be weary, but I never forgot you—your love or your kisses. I went forth in the morning to labor. Perhaps it is but little we have, but, thank God, darling, it was honestly won; we love each other and are happy. I try to be good and honest, and, guarded by your love, succeed. And no temptation yet met has won me from my vows and from you; no place has lured me from my home and the loved; no wish have I had for something beyond the confines of my happy dominion. All the day, and all the week I have *toiled there*, as you have *cared here*, and see, darling, how our home grows more and more beautiful as your taste displays the little things purchased with the earnings of my hand and brain.

"God bless you, darling, and make me always good, and kind, and true, and earnest, and deserving of the love you give me. Here is my *home;* here is my *heart;* here is my *treasure;* here I live as there I labor, and every hour not given to toil is to thee and happiness. And as I go I will think of thee; of the time when you said "Yes" to my wooing; and never will I do that which would pain your heart, and then I shall ever be happy, and love you alone, my darling, queen of my heart-warmed home."

And her hand presses mine; her eyes are like rays from the eternal, as she looks the words tongue cannot speak. Her lips are so sweet and warm, so full of that wondrous electricity which all know not of; her cheek rests on my shoulder, and from her heart, from her loved lips, come these words:—

"God bless you, darling, for your manhood and its unsullied bringing. The day has not been long, for I *knew* you would hasten. And I was happy, as here and there my hands found employment. And see how nicely I have fixed this, and that; for thus you like them, as thus I fixed them. And, darling, I am *so glad* you have been good and true to us both. I am glad if my love is the shield that keeps you from falling when tempted, as we all are. You have toiled all the day, now rest with me,— on this breast, by these lips, in this heart of mine, for all are yours. Come, darling, to the feast, and none so sweet as by love alone invited! You are home, where all is yours, with never a regret, or a wish for another. I love *you*, darling, and I pray Him above to give us hearts to know *our treasures*,— to know who are the truly rich; and I pray Him to spare us to enjoy all there is that is truly beautiful in life till we rest again united where there is no Saturday Night.

VII.

About a Little Girl Whose Name is Lulu.

JUST the faintest little tap at the door.
"*Come in!*"

Sitting in an easy-chair, watching the burning coke in the grate making faces, and half-listening to conversation, we were thinking of the poor ones who had no easy-chairs and cheery fires. The door opened slowly; with hesitating step there entered a young girl of eleven years.

"Please, do you want to buy some hooks and eyes?"

"No, I guess not," said a gentleman, who was busy in another part of the room.

"Please, I sell them very cheap, and my mother is very poor."

And while he was calling the attention of the good-hearted lady of the house, we took up the conversation:

"Come here, little girl."

And she came,— a sweet-faced, modest little thing, in her hand a little paper box.

"What have you to sell?"

"Hooks and eyes, and a belt-buckle."

"Not much of stock, have you?"

"No, sir, not much; for we are too poor."

"How do you sell them?"

"Five cents a card."

"It is after dark; isn't it late for little girls to be out?"

"Yes, sir; but we have no other time."

"Who is *we?*"

"My little sister; she is nine years old."

Another faint little teeny tap at the door.

"*Come in!*"

And in came the little sister, with a smaller box. She was a pretty little child,—her eyes seeming just like the eyes of a dear little pet who calls us papa, and kisses us such loving welcome, and whose years are no more than the little one's before us.

"Come here, little one."

And she came and stood beside her sister. Who could help putting his arm around her little innocent form, and drawing her closer to him? She had no silks, but her face and eyes were enough to win any heart.

"Come, sit on our knee. Now, tell me all about it. What is your name?"

"Lulu.

"That is a pretty name. I like it. Where is your papa?"

"He was killed in the army, in a battle."

"Where is your mother?"

"She lives in a room on East Eleventh Street, sir."

"What does she do?"

"She sews when she is able to and can get any work."

"Is she sick sometimes?"

"Yes, sir, a good deal. And she can't support all of us."

"How many little ones has she?"

"Three, sir,—my brother, who is thirteen, my sister, and I."

"What does your brother do?"

"He has a place in a store, and earns two dollars a week."

"Does he board at home?"

"Yes, sir."

"And you and your sister sell little things?"

"Yes, sir; after we get through helping mother, we sell about one hour each evening."

"How much have you sold to-night?"

"Fourteen cents' worth."

"How much have you sold?"—to the sister.

"Thirty-five cents, sir, with what you paid me."

"Quite a trade. Now, I want a card of hooks and eyes to comb my hair with, and a belt buckle to put on my wrist."

The little girl said it was funny, and sold us the articles, when the conversation was resumed:

"What does your mother sew on?"

"She embroiders and makes aprons and little things for any one who wants her to."

"Is she very poor?"

"Yes, sir; we didn't have any bed, nor stove, nor furniture, when we moved in where we live now."

"When was that?"

"This winter."

"Was it cold?"

"Yes, sir; we nearly froze some nights; but we slept close together, and mamma took care of us.

"Do you go to school?"

"No, sir."

"Why not?"

"Please, sir, I have no clothes good enough to wear. But mamma will get me some, some day, and I wont look so ragged, and can go."

"Can you read?"

"Yes, sir, in the third reader."

"Well, Lulu, tell your mamma when she is ready to send you to school to have you come here, and I will buy you all the little clothes you want for one year, for you put me in mind of another little girl."

And the good lady where we were that evening said also,—

"Yes, Lulu, he will do it, for he said he would; and I'll make you a nice little hat to wear."

And two little tears came into her eyes as she tried to say, "Thank you."

Looking upon a fruit-basket filled with oranges on a centre-table, we wondered if she had had any lately, and asked,—

"Have you had any oranges lately?"

"Yes, sir; a gentleman gave me one a good while ago."

"Here is money to buy a nice one for your brother, your sister, and your mamma, and yourself."

She dropped her head as if thinking, and then, furtively looking us in the face, said,—

"*Please, sir, I'd rather buy some cakes for supper.*"

"Haven't you been to supper?"

"No, sir."

Then we thought how just like a man it was to

not think, and asked where she lived more particularly. And she told us,—a few doors east of Second Avenue, on Eleventh Street, just opposite a neat little bakery, where she could get the cakes.

Putting on hat and overcoat, with the two little ones we went down stairs from the cheerful room into the street, to find, first the bakery, then the mother. And the little ones told us how their papa was killed in battle; how they once had a plenty. And little Lulu said God was the best friend she had, and her mother next. She said God would always care for the poor if they would trust him, and that she prayed to him every night. And she went to Sunday-school, and tried to be a good little girl.

Here was perfection of faith; and we could not help thinking that the blessed Jesus, when on earth, could not help saying, "Suffer little children to come unto me, and forbid them not, for of such is the kingdom of heaven."

We found the bakery, and a pleasant-voiced woman waiting on customers therein. Then we crossed directly over the street into a tenement house, and, guided by the little ones, found the room where they lived. And we found a middle-aged women, worn with care. But she was good — her eyes and her face and her words told it. She made aprons and all such work. And she told us, a stranger, that once she lived in Lodi, Seneca County, New York; that her husband was a music-teacher. And then she told us that he went South for his health; was drafted into the Southern army, and killed in battle. Then she came North, destitute of all save her little ones and faith in God.

Then we asked Lulu to bring us an apron for a lady the next afternoon at five o'clock, and went out into the busy street, and from there to meet in council brethren of the mystic tie.

And all the night we were in dreamland; and pure-eyed little girls were, with tears in their eyes, trying to say "*Thank you,*" or were nestling by our side. The next day we left the city for the West, two hours earlier than we intended, and did not see Lulu. But she did not forget us, as the following extract from a letter will show:

"251 East Thirteenth Street, New York City, *April* 13.

· · · "Little Lulu came promptly at five o'clock, with a beautiful apron made expressly for you and in her sweet little hand a pink she had bought for you. She felt quite disappointed at not seeing you. But Lizzie bought the apron for you and appropriated the pink. She came again, last night, with another apron, which I sold for her, for two dollars to a gentleman below. She says when you return she will come and see you."

Saturday Night.—The hand on the watch-dial before us near twelve. Sitting by the bedside of a sick friend, we write this in lieu of our usual reveries. It is a simple little story we have told above, exactly as it occurred, as any one can learn. And from our other city in the West, we write, wondering where is the little Lulu, and if her faith in God is still the same. And we think of the thousands and tens of thousands that are of God's poor who are uncared for. Children of working-men and working-women; little orphans, who never know of parental love; little wanderers to eternity, who have no one to buy them oranges, cakes, dolls, playthings, or keepsakes.

In thought to-night we have been far away, looking into tenement houses; into garrets, cellars, and hovels; into little beds in orphan asylums; looking into the faces of the poor and the innocent who battle daily with fate. How few there are who know how others suffer — few there are who care. God bless the Christian mother who suffers; who taught her little ones to pray, and who is winning a crown to wear in the beautiful Eternal Land.

And we have all the night been thinking of the ones who profess to be Christians and to care for their fellow-men; who spend thousands of dollars for fashionable churches, cushioned pews, swell ministers, and solid silver or gold communion service. Little do they care for the poor and the needy. Their eyes look up the tall steeples they have built, but seldom down to the bare feet and ragged garments of the "tears of God" that plead for care and notice. We love the poor and do not care for the rich. We have no money for spires with gilded domes, or tinkling inventions to suspend therein, nor for high-priced pews, with elastic backs and velvet trimmings. Time enough for these when we turn hppocrite and from softness of brain try to deceive Deity by studying a fashion book rather than kneeling before Him in earnest, secret prayer.

Be kind to the poor! They have few friends on earth — especially if they be white. God made them white; they are not to blame! Christians pray for them, then over church doors write, "No admittance here!" They erect elegant sleeping places for themselves, while drowsy ministers are spinning their cant and style, but never think of beds for the little ones who are homeless. They visit caucuses, visit election places, visit political meetings, but have no time to dry tears or mellow the hearts of those who need sympathy.

To all the mothers, we say, "Have faith." And to all our little friends, who read this, those words: "Think how good your fathers and mothers are to you, and rejoice that you have a home and some one to love you, and always speak kindly to the poor, even if you can give nothing to make them happier, and we shall be glad to know that if we have done no good, at least we have done no harm or wrong this Saturday Night.

VIII.

Such a Little Coffin!

IT was not twice the length of the sheet of paper on which we write this article!

A little coffin—a little bit of a coffin, not large enough to contain half the playthings a little girl we know of has to amuse herself with.

It was not a casket, or burial case with silver

handles, white satin, silver fringe, and glass skylight to the home of the departed. All these are for the rich men—the bondholders, whose children are said to be better than the little children of working-men. It was simply a little plain coffin made from black walnut, and it was being carried into a house on Canal Street as we walked home this Saturday Night, very weary, from our work.

No one else noticed it. A poor man came to the door when the undertaker rang the bell. He looked sad and lonely, just as thousands we know would look if a little coffin should be wanted in their homes to-night! Hundreds hurried by; who of them thought of the mourners?

Slowly we walked home. Somebody was in the depths of sorrow. Who it was we knew not. We could not keep from thinking, and after supper we went back to the house and rang the bell. The man, with a sad face, came to the door.

"Good evening, sir. Can a stranger, who means well, be of service to you?"

"Oh! thank you; but it is not much a stranger or a friend can do. Who are you? Why come you here? We have never met."

"Simply a friend. I have nothing to do; I saw the little coffin come in; perhaps I can do some good—and I felt like coming. That is all."

"Oh, sir, you are welcome! But it is all sadness here now. Come this way."

And we walked into a little room where the little coffin was. A little boy, not four years born, rested there. The coffin was on a table. The sweet little face, so waxen and fair, did not seem like death, but for the little rosebud beside the pale temple. The great, big tears came down so fast over the brown face of our friend, — for, if in trouble he was our friend, — as he said, —

"He was our only treasure, and we did *so* love him."

"Where is his mother?"

"She is sick, sir, — worn out with nervous excitement, — and is in our room, almost heart-broken."

And we found her weeping bitterly, and as we sat by the side of the lounge on which she reclined, we could only say, "Indeed, I am very, very sorry for you." And we saw a little pin on his bosom, till then unnoticed.

"Are you a Mason?"

"I am, or I try to be one."

"Well, brother, the light in the East is still bright; those are the most favored who are earliest called from labor to refreshment.

. . . .

Just a little coffin. No one would notice it in a city like this. The hearse passes along, a few carriages try to keep up as the driver hurries through the tangled teams and over horse-car tracks. Then he stops, a jam of carriages is formed, and a policeman says, in a coarse voice, "Move on, move on!" He might have seen it was but a little coffin and spoken a little more kindly. No one could have spoken so harshly who mourned. The omnibus with its load, hurried by; a carriage, filled with laughing ladies, hurried by, and those on its cushioned seats never cared to look at the little coffin even for one little minute. A drayman saw what it was and kindly waited a moment; his eyes seeming to say, "I am sorry for somebody."

And so they bore it away over the river. The hearse on the ferry-boat stood beside a market wagon, on which the driver sat whistling an opera air. A dandy-looking swell stood with cane in hand, one foot on the hub of the hearse, looking with half-satisfied eye on the pretty ankle of a girl who was leaning and looking over the railing of the boat. The coffin was not so small as the ankle, but he could not see it.

And when we reached the other side, all hurried off. The crowed jammed, and men swore. Some went this way, some that.' We never saw their faces before, as we remember —never shall again! But somebody will see them some day. They will be in coffins, looking up to Him who sees little coffins as well as big ones. If this had been a big one; if there had been four horses with nodding plumes, a silver-trimmed casket, instead of a plain little coffin, a long string of carriages, half-empty,— folks would have asked who it was that was thus keeping ahead of us, and at tea-tables would have told the news. And folks would have asked how much money he had left; that is, how much good he might have done but did not!

But it was only a little coffin; three carriages

followed it; it was the child of a working man, but, with it, to God, went the grief-stricken hearts of those who mourned because their only joint treasure had been called home. Never mind. He who is so good is the great never-dying echo of "Suffer little children to come unto me, and forbid them not, for of such is the kingdom of Heaven." And He will always welcome the little ones to him, kiss the tears from the eyes of those who mourn, and send them back to life's duties, while He cares for the jewels in that Heaven we all hope for.

Only a little coffin! Who ever thinks of them? Little caskets contain the most precious treasures. The buds are promises of flowers; and when the bud is taken we mourn, for we do not know but it might have become the most beautiful flower of all.

God pity those who have, with tear-wet eyes looked upon little coffins. The hope of the father and the mother, the one who has so often been kissed and carressed, is no more. The hearts of those who brought it thus far are dark with grief. And down into the little grave buried with that little coffin, go a thousand hopes, dreams, castles, ideas, and links, connecting us with and drawing us on to the future. Indeed, few there are who know how much the little coffins hold! The agony of the mother who has once before suffered; the fears of the father who held her head, and by her pillow watched, with kind touch and gentle kiss; the hours of quiet talk over the future of the new guest to love's table; the hopes, fears, watchings, care and affection God gives us for the little ones,—all are packed into that coffin, till it seems as if He must love the little one just come to Him for the years of heart and hopes dashed to pieces, which come like prayers of mourners beseeching His eternal care.

Little coffins.

Little caskets.

Little treasures.

Chrysalis and Butterfly. Promise and Reward. Buds here, flowers there. Little graves here, little crowns there. The little coffins are dear, for there we gave to rest our little and our loved ones. And where they sleep are little hillocks, which also mark the wounds on our hearts. And the little hillocks will last after we have gone to the Eternal Land, where only can our wounds be healed!

And the little hillocks are everywhere, — city and town, cemetery and graveyard, — crowded together, and singly, they are to be found. And when we see them in the quiet cities of the dead, we feel sorry for those who there hid from sight the little coffins, and say, 'way down deep in our heart, God bless and make happy the little ones there at rest, and all who mourn that they are not with us, who so loved them, and carried to them presents, and love, and kisses, and kind words every Saturday Night.

IX.

Kind Words from Woman's Lips.

AGAIN has the angel folded up the book of seven daily chapters, and stored it away with the thousands of volumes waiting God's opening thereof, when He will be ready to examine our records after our final Saturday Night has come and we live but in memory. All the week we have been working and thinking. We have watched the little tin pails spoken of in a former chapter, go and come, and seen many a man with one in his hand turn his eyes to look at our office as he passed by, and step in to purchase the paper wherein we spoke of his silent morn, noon, and night companion.

And to-night we relate a little incident, not much of itself, but volumes for all. The man of whom we write will pardon us for this article, for telling to thousands of others the simple tear-wet story he told us as he sat in a chair by us, his little tin pail on the floor beside him. He was a great, strong man — strong enough to have thrown us out the winpow upon the gas-lamp below; but his frame trembled, and his lip quivered as he spoke.

"My work is done for the day. I want to talk with you as a friend, and I thank you for giving me this opportunity. My name is —— Adams. I work in a foundry on —— Street. I read your article about little tin pails, and all the men in the shop heard me read it at noon. It was a good chapter, and they wanted me to thank you for writing it, for it told just what we felt. We are working-men; our hands are hard and grimed, but our hearts are warmer than many who sneer at us. The sledge, the file, the sand, the hot iron and the cold, leave their marks on us, but we think, and work, and think. And when a man speaks for us we love him.

"But it is not of this to-night. You have troubles of your own—all have. But I wish to tell you I work hard and try to save. I love my wife. Years ago, when she was younger than now, I loved her; and I have always tried to make her happy. We had no home then, as we have now. I worked and earned our home; these hands and these muscles earned it. It is not a rich home, but it is ours, and sometimes very happy.

"Sometimes when I go home I am very tired. It is hard work to labor as we have to. And some days I am sick and tired, and my head aches, and my bones ache, and I do not feel strong. But I work, for we must eat. Her and the babes must eat and be clad. And I go home tired. And sometimes she is glad to see me, and sometimes she is cross and scolds. She says I do not love her, when I do. And she seems not to care for me And she speaks hot, sharp, bitter words. They would not hurt if others said them, but when they come from her lips, I feel sick and tired of life. I try to be good and kind, and mean to do right. All the way from the shop, I wonder if she will be kind or cross when I reach home. Sometimes she is real good, and her eyes look so loving, and her hand feels so warm and full of life as she places it in mine!

Then my heart grows big, and full, and brave, and I could die for her or go back to the shop, tired as I am, and work all night for her and for them. And then I am so happy, and our home is so happy; the evening is so short I wonder where it went to! And we lay our heads on the same pillow, and sleep close to each other, loved and loving.

"But, pshaw! why do I tell you this? I would not, but something tells me you know it all.

"And sometimes I go home, and she is not so kind. And there is not one bit of love-light in her eyes, and she seems so cold! If I am sick and tired, I could almost sink. Of course she does not know how hard I toiled all day. The hours go by slowly sometimes. And when she is cross I am cross. We eat our supper in silence, and I go out. And I walk the street, looking at windows and envying those who are happier than I. And I go to some place where drink is sold, and instead of taking a social glass with a friend and going home early, stay and drink, and spend money, and grow reckless, and don't care, and stay out till midnight, for I hate to go home when it is not pleasant there.

"Don't blame us who drink at times. We dont want to; but sometimes — sometimes, you know, our home ones do not give us kind words, and we feel heart-sick. Sometimes I stop for a moment to take a glass of ale, or beer, or something warm, with a friend. We have worked hard all day, and think we need it, whether we do or not. And we talk a few minutes, for it is little talk we do in the shop. And then she scolds, and gives me red-hot words, and they burn and blister. She says I do not love her, when I do. And she scolds me for spending a dime or so, and acts as if I were the slave and she the monarch, and it drives me sick and crazy, and I don't care what I do.

"To-night I am going home. I shall be a little late, but never mind. I wanted to see you — our friend — and to thank you, and to ask you to write more such articles, for they make us better. And I'll read them every Saturday Night while I live. I must go now. Good-night."

God bless that man! — that worker. He told us his story, simple and plain, as we have given it, and we give it to-night to others knowing that many a good man has been driven to ruin by the one who might have saved him by using kind words.

It is hard to labor all day. When night comes the mind is nervous; hard words are like molten potash to the weary husband and father, who has been annoyed and bothered all day long. Good wife, we would see you happy, and in behalf of those who are working to make homes and to care for you, we ask for more kind words, for they are the sunshine of life, which will make home cheerful and happy, be it never so humble or lowly. Try them for a week, if no longer, and commence with this Saturday Night.

X.

Staggering Home.

GOD knows we are sorry for him! For five minutes we have watched him from our window. A stout young man, apparently thirty years of age. He looks like a working-man. We should say a man of family. See! steady there, with hand against the iron fence in front the house, step by step, staggering along. Take care there—almost down. Now he crawls and staggers on.

His clothes are muddy, as if somebody had been spattering him. His face looks haggard and distressed. He is *going home*. Great God! what a visitor to some earnest woman and little children waiting his coming, and here it is half-past eleven o'clock at night! Poor fellow! going to ruin because it is fashionable. Here comes a kind policeman.

"Halloa, old fellow! what ails your legs?"

"Tired—very tired."

"Where you live?"

"No. — Second Avenue."

"Well, come along; I'll help you home."

"And you wont take me in?"

To *take in* means to take to the police station.

"No, if you come along quietly. This is no place for a drunken man."

"All—right—I'm yer friend?"

Arm in arm they went away. We do not know who that poor fellow is, whose home is hardly reached; but he is *somebody*. He had a mother, and how her heart would have mourned to have seen him thus! Perhaps it is to his mother's house he is going. Perhaps to his own home, if a drunkard's place of living can be called a *home*. If to a wife and children that policeman is leading him, God pity them. Doubtless he has worked all the week. Most likely some good fellow, who is kind, and gentle, and loving, when sober. But now, what is he? A poor, weak, helpless man, unable to care for himself. A sorrow and shame to his loved ones, a disgrace to himself.

We do not know how much money it cost him to win this prize. But it cost something. Perhaps a dollar. Perhaps less. Better have thrown the money away and kept his manhood.

Better have given his dimes to the little beggar children. Better have bought a little picture or picture-book for his children; a picture for his walls; a better hat than the one he wore; a pair of shoes or stockings for the little ones, who love him for all he goes down into such helplessness to their neglect; or a present for the wife who so often has cared for him in these plights, and who to-night will weep and mourn, and feel so discouraged, as she washes and combs and cares for the one she cannot help loving, for all his foolish weakness.

God only knows what a true wife and mother suffers when her husband and the father of her babes has no honest pride and love of family to make him care for his home ones. And God pity the poor man who has given his heart in exchange for that eating, craving, burning thirst for stimulants, knowing there is no safety under their influence. Every week he lowers himself deeper into the terrible well. He has friends, so-called, while his money lasts. But one by one his dollars go. Little by little his hope fades out. His pluck and ambition become dull and blunted. He cares for nobody. His employer does not want an unsteady man, and pretty soon he has lost his place. A good workman, but too unsteady. The downward road is easier to travel. Blueness, or depression of spirits follow; the home he has not made beautiful loses its attractions; the wife is found often in tears, while sighs from a grief-laden heart tell that she lingers in the shadow of better days to dread the terrible future with a drunken husband.

Once he was kind, and good, and manly. His eye never was clouded or dazed in its look. His lips were not dry and parched. His tongue was not thick. His breath was not so poison-laden and offensive. He lived other than in his throat.

If he would only listen to us. Once we were very, very poor, even penniless. But we worked and saved. We saw what money would and could do; that it bought pretty things for places of dissipation and made them attractive. And we saw that men loved to be in attractive places. And for fear we would be sick and without money we worked. And to make our home attractive we saved our earnings, till at last we made a sanctum more beautiful than any room we ever saw, and people asked how we did it.

By saving our earnings and putting the money we might have spent in dissipation, in pictures, paintings, carpets, desks, sofas, tables, curtains, and little works of art. Thus we gave employment to working-men. We purchased the result of others' labor with the result of our own. We encouraged mechanics and art-workers, made our home attractive. Every dollar thus invested helped make a wall between us and dissipation.

Once in Milwaukee, at a ball, a nice young

man refused to dance in the set we were in because we were poor. He was rich, or his father was. He thought nothing of expending five, ten, twenty, or even fifty dollars a night, treating his companions. He was a good fellow. He was popular with girls and boys. Years passed. One day a bloated-faced man called at our Western office.

"Don't you know me?"

"No; and yet we have met somewhere!"

"Quite right; I knew you in Milwaukee. Times have changed since then. You have grown rich; I am poor, and no one cares for me now. I want some work; I have no money, — have eaten nothing to-day."

"You are —— ——, but how changed!"

"Yes, I am he. And you will help me, wont you?"

"Have you a trade?"

"No; I never learned one."

"No one cares for you now; *do you care for yourself?*"

"Don't ask me!"

"Where are your *old friends,*— the boys you were so popular with?"

"Oh, they have gone to the devil, or those who have not, have gone back on me — quit when I had no more money. But tell me how you got this fine office. When I knew you a few years ago, you were poor."

"Well, I'll tell you. What you invested in dissipation I invested in books, pictures, and machinery. While you squandered, I saved. While you *didn't care*, I did. When I cared for myself, others cared for me."

"Well, I see it; but can you give me work?"

"No, you are not in condition to work. To give you a place I must discharge a good man, who is sober and trying to get along. This I cannot do."

Pardon this diversion, but we ran into thinking of old times, and have been counting up our boyish friends, to know how many of them have succeeded, and the result makes us sad.

We do wish the working-men would be more careful of their earnings. They would be so much happier, have better homes, be better loved, and we should not have had the chapter to have written we have this Saturday Night.

XI.

Worth of Woman's Love.

ONLY *another* week! How short it has been! seven days — seven chapters of light and happiness, of joys and sorrows, of hopes and fears, of trials and conquests, of births and marriages, of sickness and of health. But a little thing is a week; but it is a life to some, in the results it doth bring.

To-night we were made to feel sad, yet happy. On the way home we passed a woman in calico, leading by the arm a weak, tottering, trembling old man. His step was hardly a step; he could hardly lift his feet from the pavement; his face was wrinkled with the lines of ninty-one winters, while his scattered hairs were silky and white as the purest snow.

And the woman was past the fifty. Her face was kind; her eyes told volumes. The crowd on the Bowery turned aside as it hurried by to let the old man toddle on.

"Good evening, good woman; can we help you?"

"Oh, no, thank you!" And she looked so kindly at us. "We are almost home — a few steps farther; and you are in a hurry, — going home too, perhaps."

Almost Home!

Yes, the old man, who little heeded the crowd, and who looked with mazed and puzzled gaze on the busy scene, was almost home! A few more Saturday Nights and he will be there with Him, and then he can walk, and run without stumbling or other support than His.

And we passed on, to think, and think. And we thought of woman's love, and the worth of it. How she cared for him — we should think her father. Perhaps he was cross and petulant years ago, if not now; yet she was kind to him, and with care steadied his steps lest he fall and the busy crowd trample him under feet. And we thought of thousands and thousands of good women in different places, who love, are good, and true, and pure, and kind; who deserve happiness here and Heaven hereafter.

All over the land we saw them as we walked home. The entire line of clouds seemed to be rolled back by some great hand as somebody said, "Look at them everywhere."

And we did look into thousands of homes, — by the farmer's fire, and in the woodman's cabin;

by the sick bed and kneeling with grief-laden hearts and tear-wet faces, beside corpses and coffins. We saw them in calico and homespun by thousands, and they all told of woman's worth, love, and devotion.

Little do men know of woman's sorrows, heartaches, hungerings for love, temptations, and resistings. Men go and come. They are busy. Avenues of labor and amusement are opened to them, for they have power to open to suit themselves. They plunge into business, engage in enterprises, hunt, fish, sport, idle, dissipate, go and come, mixing, talking, eager to be interested. When tired, they rest; but woman's work is never done, and she must labor on, a prisoner within close walls, like a caged bird seeing the world but not mixing therewith lest she be lost.

We know of a home where a woman works cheerfully, for he she loves works like us. She wears calico, and knows nothing of opera. Her heart is in her home, her loved ones; she is happy, for they all live for her as she does for them. And oh, the wondrous depth of her love! She is by the bedside, the table, the chair, everywhere. She is monarch of home—queen of hearts; and willing tributes do her subjects pay.

Her hand stills pain; her lips greet with such pure, earnest, loving kisses! Her words are ever so kind and gentle while her life is not lost in selfishness. She is not a vain beauty, cold as marble, indifferent to others, caring only for herself, for position and the outward adornment of her person, tyrannizing over hearts compelled by the ukase of society to pay vows where none are due. But she is a good woman—a loving woman. A loving, affectionate, gentle, caressing woman a man always loves, and is willing to care for, protect and defend.

We love a good, warm-hearted woman. Not one of these simple beauties who are gay, painted, padded, befrixed and befrizzled adornings of fashion, without heart or true worth. Such are very nice to look upon, good to flirt with, nice to take to the opera, the races, the theatre, or to skirmish with when the coast is clear and willing ones seek for adventure, but they don't wear for keeps like the good, plain, sensible women who have hearts and whose worth is more than pen or tongue can tell.

Women would be better and happier if men loved them better and were more true to them. If men would strive as much to make home happy as they do to seek happiness elsewhere, the world would be better.

Hours do come when men admit the power the worth of woman. Not in sunshine so much as in shade and storm. When engrossed with business and rolling on the sea of success, we too often forget the ones without whom life would be a blank, and only fly to the havens and shelters, the love and gentle caresses of woman, when the waves are high and to remain abroad is to perish.

Then comes the hour when all admit the power of the weak. It is the care of woman which makes millions of homes beautiful, and makes love's palaces of laborers' cabins and farmers' cottages. It is the love we have for woman,— the love they have for us as men,— that drives us ahead to conquests and victories. The words kindly spoken, the smile of those we love, the commendation of those we respect of women, make men of all who are not debased, and draw our hearts to them with irresistible power. And as we see them day after day patiently, earnestly toiling to help others walk; as we see them leading the weak, aiding the unfortunate, and by the wondrous power of their God-given love, and the magic of their smiles, caresses, and prayers, we wonder that all men do not pay more tribute to the worth of woman's love.

Theirs is not the forum nor the hustings. We do not love those who strive for masculinity. But the good women, — the plain earnest, home women of the land, regardless of church or sentiment political, we would see all men more attentive and kind to, for our happiness ends in their love, as the week ends in Saturday Night.

XII.

Funeral Next Door.

IN the great city made by man!
"*Funeral next door!*"
"Who?"
"Don't know!"

The hearse stands with rear end to the house. Four horses, with nodding plumes, wait the coming of the corpse and the order of the undertaker to go ahead. Carriages line the *trottoir*, or sidewalk, waiting to take up the mourners and the expectants. Down the steps they come, pall-bearers with the coffin. Silver handles, silver screw-heads, silver plate, hot-house flowers, and embroidered pall-cloth folded in hand. Now gently — all right! Steadily the little rollers on the floor of the hearse revolve, two by two the corpse-bearers step back — all in — close the door — step up a little, driver — mourners' carriages fall in — all right ahead. And away to the silent city goes the man who has just traded houses, giving the work of a lifetime as boot-money! Expression inelegant, but truth undeniable.

"*Not know who he was?*"

Of course not. He lived there; we live here. This is the city where each person minds his own business, and meddles not with the affairs of another. This is city style. The wall which divided us might have been an hundred leagues thick, but no further through than it was, so far as they and us are concerned. He was some man, or she was some woman, or it was some child. He lived up-town — down town — in a store, an office, a bank — somewhere. He might have been an ex-mayor, a millionaire, a gambler, preacher, editor, politician, statesman, speculator, knave or fool. We knew him not. He knew not us. And yet we have known him — he us. He might have been an enemy; perhaps a friend. He came at one hour, we at another. He arose early, we late. He rode or walked one way, we another.

"Did he have a family?" How do we know? Sombody lived there, next door, but we never knew nor cared. Nor they for us. Not long since there was a wedding party there. It might have been him or her who was of the party most interested. We do not know; were not invited. The other night there was dancing next door. We heard the music and the dancers as we turned the night key of our own door. And we, too, had a party, but the next door was not concerned.

The occupant of the next house may have been the best or the worst man in the world; he may have been rich or poor, happy or miserable, old or young, married or single, healthy or sickly; we know not. Perhaps he was poisoned. Maybe he killed himself. He may have died drunk; we hope, sober. He may leave a wife and little ones to weep. Mayhap, a wife to rejoice that the physician or the undertaker saved her feeing a lawyer for a divorce! Perhaps he was an old miser, whose heirs rejoice at his death. And it may be, the coffin contained one who was a wife, a mother, a sister. They live, or lived, next door to us, as we to them. They knew people —so do we. People know them, are friends to them. So we have friends—and in a dozen days, or a dozen years, might have known them and they us.

The procession has moved out of sight. The undertaker's foreman is moving off the chairs brought by him for the mourners and friends who had been called together, for he or she had more friends than chairs in the house. More friends than chairs! Let us count the chairs in our room. Sixteen and two sofas. Sixteen friends and two sofas. Who of us has sixteen friends,—we mean friends who have the pluck to stand by us, rain or shine, hot or cold, rich or poor, in luck or out? We have one friend—yes, thousands! And God bless them, as we would, if in our power.

But not of them, but of him or her who has gone. They live near, yet we know them not. So near and yet so far! And so it is in the city. They live each side of us—overhead, underneath. Yet we know them not. They may be

Christians, Jews, infidels, deists, atheists, ranters, or, worse than all, Puritans; they may be good, bad, or indifferent—we know them not. The next door may be where lives a priest, a pirate, a printer, a physician. Perhaps it is a good house—perhaps a bad one. Well, what of it? They mind their buisness. We mind ours, and never quarrel. Yet, for all this, we at times wonder who lives next door; how he lives, for whom, and why. And we wonder were they really mourners or heart swindlers who attended the funeral next door?

If we could only look in there sometimes! But then they might look in upon us! How would we like that? And so we live in the city, known and yet not known, knowing and not knowing, friends and not friends; each intent upon his or her own business, not caring whether there be parties for joy or for grief, parties for business or pleasure, parties for revelling or mourning, so near us. But

Funeral Next Door. 119

this we do know: there was a funeral next door to us, and some of these days we, too, shall be called home, and they who so near yet not so near, will, as we have done, look out the window to notice there is a funeral next door, and to mention it perhaps, if not during the week, when shall come Saturday Night.

XIII.

"Only Two Laborers Killed!"

A FEW lines told the story.

"The passengers escaped unhurt — only two laborers killed."

So the dispatch read in the paper this morning announcing a collision on the Central Railroad. Only two laborers! But wait a moment. Who

Only Two Laborers Killed. 121

were these laborers? The trains met; there was a crash; the passengers escaped unhurt, and the only ones sent or called home were two laborers. The train passed on. Passengers talked and chatted. They read books and papers, played cards, or slept. Loved ones behind them or before them, waiting their returning or coming.

Only two *laborers* killed! Who were they? What were they? Where were they? No names given—no thought. Had one of Vanderbilt's trotting horses died or been killed, the telegraph and the papers would have told full particulars; for is not the horse of a rich man of more account than the life of a laborer? A simple-minded, honest, toiling laborer?

Who was he?

We will tell you. He was a poor working-man. Day after day he toiled, early and late. Men rode over the railroad he helped build, and praised the enterprise of its managers, but never stopped to think of him who gave his health, muscle, and very life to the work. He was passed by as of less account than the little smile of a pretty girl or bewitching woman.

But he was a man. Years ago he was an infant, and rested, as do the children of others, in loving arms. There was joy at his coming years ago. There were prayers of a loving mother for his health, happiness, and escape from temptation. But where the mother is now we cannot tell; for he was but a laborer, and in the eyes of the rich they are not worth mentioning, except as cooks, washers, ironers, menders, or old women. Are they not the most blessed who die young?

Yes, she loved him, and wept when he went into the world. And her prayers followed him to protect, and he became a laborer rather than a loafer or a criminal, forgetting God and mother alike. And he toiled; and in time he loved just as we love. His hands were hard, but do you not know his heart was soft, and kind, and mellow? And by the labor of his hands he earned a little home, where to his heart he held the dear ones who wait in vain his coming.

He was a laborer—he is now at rest, for his work is done. *Somebody* mourns. The heart of *somebody* will be made very sad, for this is the first Saturday Night he has not come with his honest heart to love the dear ones of his little home. He toiled for others: such is the laborer's lot. But when comes the resting-hour, loving eyes watched his coming, listening ears waited so eagerly for the familiar step, loving lips were put up to greet him, a tired yet loving breast was pressed against his own; a heart all, all his, felt enraptured to know the laborer had returned.

Somebody loved him and them. All the week has the home one worked and waited for him and the coming of Saturday Night. Many the plans for the morrow and coming week. Many the little stories of incident to be told as head and head on pillow rested, the heart beating in love's unison the while.

Laborers love. And they have homes dear to them. And the eyes that look for their coming, the heart that feels their absence, kisses that greet them, are sweet as the dew of richer love. And when he does not come now, oh! how terribly anxious will be the waiting ones. He comes not. That is his step—no! Ah, here he comes—no, it is some one else! And you may wait, and wait; he was only a laborer, and it is not worth while to be in a hurry to tell *his* family! Perhaps it will be best to bury him and say nothing, for he was only a laborer!

But there are breaking hearts in his home, as in others. The dream of life is broken. The hopes of years, the joys of a lifetime, the dreadful and lonely future, the weight of a bitter-struck heart, now fill the place where was the laborer, whose name is not worth the space it would take in a daily paper! And you may shove back his chair from the table, return his plate to the pantry, pour out the full of his cup, leave his pillow from the bed, hang up, fold, or give away the garments he wore, search his pockets, and read the letters and papers he left at his little home—wander, oh so sad and lonely about the rooms, for he comes no more. That book he liked to read; that picture he looked at; the little presents his love-filled heart prompted giving to you, the keepsakes moss-covered with tender memories, he will never look at or talk over with you as you sit side by side; for his work is finished, he is at rest, and you who mourn are the ones we pity, and God knows how earnestly.

Perhaps they will bring him home. In a rough box; on a coarse board, with a few blood-stained clothes thrown over him; hair tossing hither and yon, eyes aglare and aglaze. Maybe they will not care to bother with a dead laborer, for he can be of no more use to the rich, and is to be hated because he left loved ones for the living to look after!

But they will bring him, and go to their suppers—you to your mourning! Then you can weep and pray. You may kneel by him, as we knelt for and to the loved and lost, till it seems as if the heart must and would break with agony. And you may look at his unspeaking face; lay your hands on that forehead; press your warm lips to his cold ones, and ask God to take you also: this you can do, if he was but a laborer!

Thank God the rich, who hold our notes as bonds which we must pay, cannot keep us from loving each other, nor from paying tribute to trusting hearts. Nor can they keep the ones who labor from loving each other truly, if their hands be hard, homes poor, and raiment scant. And if the rich do not care for us, we who are workingmen and laborers can care for each other, and live more for the dear ones who will mourn for us when we, too, are called to that rest which awaits us, not only here, where those who are but laborers are unnamed and unhonored, but in that better land where the rich are not our masters, and where there is no Saturday Night.

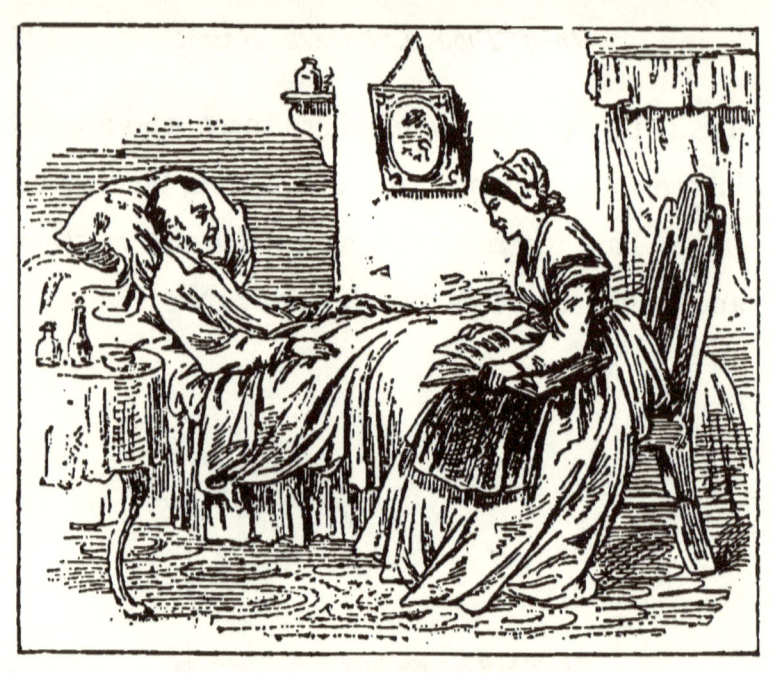

XIV.

Sinking to Rest.

ANOTHER week has been called in. Another seven-day net of Providence's has been reeled upon the invisible, and its wondrous haul of good deeds and bad pass in review before the Power of powers, the Great Father of all. A few more Saturday Nights for us—perhaps no more for many who will read this article; it may be no more for the weary, hard, and tired brain but for which this little summing up would not be made.

It is good to rest, and we are glad to have one night of the week for review — one night in which to look back at the hollowness of life — one little season in which we can look at the beautiful of it; for there is beauty in it, though the terrible to-morrow, which promises more than it brings, sadly hides the perfection of days, life, and events.

Since last we sat by the desk to write thus outside of politics or business, there have been many changes. Many a heart has been widowed, and many a sad pillow in the final earthly home marks where sleep the missed ones. Do you know there is something very strange about this life and death? We do not see why people so desire to live. From the cradle to the grave it is but toil, labor, sorrow, disappointment, and vexation. Were it not that we look for to-morrow to bring us happiness, or next week or next year to bring us comfort, there would be but dark clouds over all of us. The days, the years, are but the seconds and moments of God! That of time we prize so highly is of no moment to Him, and yet how we hang on the great pendulum, with its fifty-two figures thereon, each like this of which we write!

Death is not dreadful. It is but the sleeping here to waken there! It is but sinking to rest in our office, when wearied with the labors of the day, and waking at home, where about us will stand, in the sunshine of God's wondrous love, the dear ones gone before to prepare the parlor of Eternity for our use and our resting, forever! And who would fear to thus sleep — to lay by the pen, to shove back from the desk, and say, "Good-by, wearying labors; we part forever;" to recline the head on back of cushioned chair, to smile as our eyes see the loved ones waiting, and to know that instead of walking we are wafted silently and on wings of love, lest we waken before the glad surprise!

Working-man and brother! we care not what your language, or how much you differ from us in opinion, to you we talk to-night. Opinions are but opinions. We may be wrong, you may be wrong; each of us may be wrong; for none but God is right. You have a right to your ideas, we have a right to ours; for they are all born of a higher power, to be operated on by acts, events, and arguments. But we would add to your happiness here. Another will care for you in the Hereafter, as He will care for all of us. You teach us, by your daily example, many things. We see you nobly striving, and would help you, if such thing can be.

We all seek happiness. Let us see how it can be had. You are tired. Then rest. Go home and be with those who are with you and of you. Throw your labor and dignity behind you. Open your heart. Talk of the beauties of the past you have seen, and congratulate yourselves that so much misery which has befallen others has escaped you. No matter how hard your lot, some one has a harder one. Think if there are not near you those you would not, on any account, change places with.

If you love, love more. If you hate, hate less. Life is too short to spend in hating any one. Why war against a mortal who is going the same road with us? Why not expand the flower of life and happiness, by learning to love, by teaching those who are near and dear the beautiful lesson? Your hands may be hard, but your hearts need not be! Your forms may be bent or ugly, but do you not know that the most beautiful flowers often grow in the most rugged, unsheltered places?

The palace for care, the cottage for love. Not that there is no love in the mansion; but somehow, if we are not very careful, business will crowd all there is of beauty out of the heart. This is why God has given us Sabbaths and Saturday Nights, that we may leave business in the office, and have a heart-cleaning.

Forgive, as you would be forgiven. Love as you would be loved. Do as you would be done by. Suppose you were a weary prisoner at home, and think how welcome would be the coming of her you love, to be with you one night, if not each night, and go by the places of dissipation, of wickedness, where people would not so congregate if they did not forget! If you would have home happy, try to make it so. Light the lamp of life and keep it filled with the oil of love, care, affection, tenderness, and caresses, that it may not go to sleep in the dark when the work of life is ended. Children often fear to go to sleep in the dark; but there is another sleep, and a more terrible darkness! Only this, and nothing more!

Suppose we fall asleep in the office this Saturday Night, and, neglecting to have trimmed our lamp, awaken to find but darkness and gloom and uncertainty? We may find matches, but of what avail if there be no oil? We may die and live again; but if there be no lamps of love to lighten our future, better that we lived, even in sorrow.

Home can be happy if we make it so. Do not expect to cull all the flowers. Do not, simply to please yourself! We repeat: do not, simply to please yourself; for therein lies the shroud of happiness? Give as is given. Keep back the bitter words. Others may be weary and bitter. Words unspoken are never remembered!

Go home to-night. If you would be happy,

go home. If there is no happiness there, take some and kindle more. Save your earnings. Beautify your resting-places. Keep your heart warm and your brain steady. Save rather than waste, for the days go by faster than we dream, and want may overtake us, as it has others who lost the week in the great whirlpool of Saturday Night.

XV.

Standing before the Minister.

Saturday Night, and they have long been our friends. So they invited us.

Merely a little private affair. Him and her, and five invited guests. Twenty-four to nineteen, and they love each other.

It was not a grand wedding; that is, there was no line of carriages, diamond-glittered sensation-seekers called friends. No army of waiters, bridesmaids, musicians, ushers; no saloon and lunch-room in the back parlor; no grand splurge as if no one had married before!

But there were, it seemed to us, angels in the air, as, hand in hand, they stood before the minister, with eyes looking down as if to see the heart, they said "Yes," and with beautiful faith in the future began the wondrous voyage on that ocean thick with wrecked hopes and life's rinsings!

They were lovers.

They are man and wife.

They were and are our friends.

They begin life as we did years ago, homeless and houseless, but blessed with health, pluck, and a will to work. When the ceremony of marriage was over, we shook each by the hand, and wished them well. But we did not kiss the bride. We would not wish every spectator to kiss our new bride. Custom compels brides to submit to be kissed at this time by every comer, as men take a last look at a corpse. Confound such custom! The bridegroom stands to see his wife in the arms or hands of others —then takes to his bosom his dream of purity, her lips pounded and flavored with various breaths, liquors, and brands of tobacco. Not any for us!

The bride, a good, plain, honest, dark-eyed, sensible woman, asked, "Will you tell me how to always be as happy as now?"

"Yes: always be so!"

. . . .

It is late to-night. We have been thinking how to help our young friends. The greatest help we ever had was from an earnest friend, who gave us good advice; and we thanked him for it. So we, to-night, before sleeping, answer the question of the bride.

You are young. You wish to be happy. That is like a toy passed to each generation!

We all wish the same. There is no particular secret about it. If you want a wife, you work to win her. If you want a husband, you act, dress, and talk to please him. This is well. As you do this, so does your love grow and fasten. If you want an education, study brings it. If you want influence, you work for it. If you want happiness, plan and work for it. Don't neglect twice to care for once. Even our chronometer, reliable to a second, month after month, must be wound up, *kept running*, and thus is always to be relied on. So with happiness. Keep it running. Don't let it grow cold. Like iron molten in blast-furnaces and allowed to cool, there is no getting it out except by aid of cold-chisel and drudgery, or the destruction of the furnace. It is hard to disturb a dream and begin where you left off. So with love.

Be kind to each other. *Never* speak a harsh word to the loved one. Never speak while in anger. Hot words, like hot iron, leave a scar long after the iron has been taken away. Bear with each other. Strive to make each other happy. See who can do the most in this way, and be the best. Do not order as if he or she were a dog or a slave. Thank with words, with kisses, with looks of love for little acts, favors, and kindness. Coax, but never drive one out of the blues, depression of spirits, or sombre thoughts. Here is love's great mission. Respect the feelings and passion of the other. Let your life be a trinity of love, dignity, and goodness. But do not mistake coarseness, roughness, tyranny, and that domineering *hauteur*, for dignity, as many do.

And to him who has the work to do. Be careful. Labor and save. Earn a home. You can do it, else you are not so good as other men. Do not fool away your earnings. Do not gamble till you can afford to lose. Do not spend money for drink, for then your head, your purse, your heart is robbed. Earn and save, little by little, and in a few years, a home is yours.

The dollars you might spend foolishly, if invested in clothes for your wife, would make *you* proud of her; in books, pictures or furniture, proud of your home. Take care of what you have; it gives strength and encouragement to you both. When you buy a bundle to take home, don't pawn it, throw it in the gutter, or leave it on some bar-counter. That heart is a choice bundle; don't leave it here, or you'll lose it in the hereafter.

Have faith — have pluck — work — save. Be a man; not a brute, but a man. Be kind to your home ones; be with them all you can; take them with you all you can. Let them know that *you* take more interest in them than all others. Leave your head in your office, store, or shop; take your heart home. Romp and unbend from care; it wont hurt you one bit. Dress-parade is hard work. Keep sober; then you know what you are about, and others will respect you at all times, and your family will be proud of you, and you will be proud of yourself. Try to be somebody, and you will be apt to succeed. Give not grudgingly of love, or kind words, or comforts. All there is of life is what we get out of it to make us happy. Think of her you love at home. The days are long to her. Day after day she cooks, scrubs, cares for you and the little ones, washes, irons, mends, thinks and wishes, and hopes and fears. Don't let her lose confidence in you. Life with one in whom you have not perfect confidence is hell.

And to you who said "yes" to his wooing. Be good and love him. Let politics alone. Make home happy. Keep clean and neat. Try to make your room or your home happy. Don't scold, nor pout, nor sulk, nor be continually looking into pockets and letters for some evidence of something you would like to find.

Have confidence in him, and he will not be so apt to deceive you. Help him to live within your means. Pay no attention to dress and style beyond your ability. People care less for us all than we imagine. Dress plainly, neatly, in taste. More attention to the heart than the hair.

Then try to live for each other. This is about all there is of life. You can be happy in a cabin as in a palace, if you will only try to make your heart right. The only real home we have on earth is in the heart, the arms, or the presence of those we love, and no one can occupy two rooms at the same time. Enjoy that which you have, and thank God that you live, are loved, and have a home in which to enjoy your love and rest from the labors of the week, when you can go to it like a monarch to his throne when comes the blessed Saturday Night.

XVI.

About Burdens, and Those Who Bear Them.

WILL *they never tire?*

Do they care nothing for any of us?

Will there never be a halt to time, or will the weeks rush by like those swift-rushing trains bearing heavy burdens on — on — on — on! leaving here and there some article, as we by the weeks are left, but ever rushing on? And as those trains rush on, driven by a power we cannot see, so move the weeks on the down-grade to Eternity, caring nothing for the ones who may be ground to atoms by the flying burden.

Let us, who are wise, look out before the train — the coming of the final week, which will grind us into endless pain if we do not step aside into places of safety.

But those burdens!

This Saturday Night we were very tired in mind and body, yet light of heart as any linnet's feather, for the work of the week was done — as we felt, well done. Not one unkind word had we spoken — not one act performed we would not have our loved ones know of — no man wronged of a penny.

Homeward, slowly walking. Men — glorious, muscular, rough-bearded, honest-faced working-men — hurried by with their little tin pails, every now and then one of them having a copy of our newspaper, bought of a newsboy or from a news-stand. One man stopped at a little fruit-stand, threw down ten cents, and said good-naturedly to the old woman,—

"Some pears, aunty. Some good ones for my little ones, and put 'em in the pail."

They filled the pail nearly half-full. We looked at him in admiration, and thought of the joke he would have on the little ones when he gave them the pail to put in its accustomed place against the Monday. He looked good natured, and we asked him,—

"How many little ones have you?"

"Four."

"Where do you live?"

"On Fourth Street."

"Can you carry more than you have in your pail?"

"What do you mean?"

"Can you carry a few things up that way for me?"

"Well, I am not in the carrying business, but I don't mind to accommodate a man."

"All right. Aunty, fill that pail full of pears. Now, if you will carry these also to your little ones, and this big Bartlett to your wife, and this one for yourself, it will be a great accommodation to me."

"Well, but — but — what for? Who are you?"

"Never mind, but take these to your babies for me, and I'll thank you; for my baby is away on a visit, and I can't take her any to-night, and it will do as well if you take them to your little ones."

And we separated. He winked, and looked, and walked on to look back over his shoulder, as did we. He was not insulted at our rudeness, for the heart knows its friends.

Then we walked on, and on, and on! The carriages rolled by, rich men sitting back against the chshions. And the omnibuses, and the street cars, and the hackney coaches, all bore away to homes those who needed rest. And the cartmen, with tired horses, passed us to homes somewhere. And the streets were full of people on foot, crowding each other, as a little girl, not six years old — a ragged, barefoot, bare-head, half-dressed little thing, with a weazenish, shrunken, famine-pinched face, — came staggering across the street, with a heavy bundle of blocks and sticks, gathered from the ruins of a building near by, where the fire had been at work yesterday. It was a load we should not have cared to lug away, but she hurried on as if being pursued.

As thought directed, we touched her shoulder and lifted therefrom the bundle, tied by a dirty cord. She sprang as if struck, and, with a tear in her eye, said, —

"Please don't, sir; I didn't mean to steal them!"

"Come here, little one."

"No, sir; I'd rather go home!"

"Come here; don't be afraid. The bundle is too big for you; we'll carry it a little way for you."

She looked at us, half in doubt, as if fearing a trick, or arrest, for they drive children away from places where chips, little blocks, and sticks, are picked up in great cities. They are valuable — worth many dollars a cord — and luxuries are not for the poor! Think of this, ye who live in the country, by timber where the poor of New York would be happy if they could gather the limbs, and chunks, and bark, and sticks that are rotting.

"What is your name?"

"Anna McRafferty, sir."

"Where do you live, Anna?"

"In Houston Street."

"Is your father alive?"

"Yes, sir."

"What does he do?"

"Nothing, sir; but mother does."

"What does your mother do, Anna?"

"She does anything she can get to do, sir. She goes out to scrub, and takes care of father."

"Is your father sick?"

"Sometimes he comes home nights sick, so sick he can't walk, and sometimes mother goes out to find him."

And she told us this as we sat on the little bundle, by a fruit-stand on the Bowery. Did you ever see a little half-starved, six-year-old girl, whose dress revealed the entire anatomy and structure of her little skeleton frame, eat pears? Did you ever see a half-starved cat or dog that had been kicked and pounded by cruel people, eat a piece of meat, gnawing into it, looking up and down, and all about, as if expecting some trick, some blow, some order to "get out"? If you who have plenty in the country, yet who are always growling, and whining, and finding fault, and worrying over your supposed poverty, could see the poor of our cities, you would deserve cursing if you did not thank God for what you have and realize that you were and are kings compared to the starved ones, the human rats and mice that literally hunt for a living in this great city.

From the Bowery into Houston Street went this "somebody's baby," bearing her great bundle. God order that no rough policeman hit her with a club, arrest her for stealing kindling, send her to prison, and win promotion from brutal headquarters! Although it is wrong to steal, the bondholder and his Government rob the poor; yet the poor must not snatch a chip or a crust and escape; for the dignity of the law—the faith of the Government must be preserved!

But on she went with her burden. And

up the Bowery we walked, thinking of those who bear great burdens, almost above their strength. God pity them all — old, young, friends or enemies. How many there are whose burdens we can see. But these are not the heaviest! Men struggling to live, to accumulate — to save enough to make home comfortable and own their own coffins!

Men struggling to escape the burden of dissipation, yet lacking the pluck to walk out from under therefrom like men.

Women with cold homes, cheerless walls, bare floors, starving children, and husbands going hellward through intoxication, leaving their home ones uncared for — their wives to beggary, their children to the street — their daughters to prostitution, the morgue, or deathhouse, and to the Potter's Field. Buds that might have blossomed, torn off and trampled into the filth of the gutter!

And the hidden burdens are the worst, for none can help us carry them, nor none can escape from them to rest. Let us be careful how we take them!

All over the land are they who bear burdens. Some of doubt, of fear, of mistrust, of disappointment, of neglect, of cruelty, of unkindness, of indifference. We close our eyes on the surface to open them to the interior of this picture of life, and see burdens in thousands of homes,—thousands of hearts,— and thank God that ours are no greater.

And this is our strength — our life. No matter what our burdens, there are heavier ones borne by others! There is no person in the world but might be worse off. No matter what *our* load, somebody, child or adult, man or woman, is bearing a heavier one, and *here* is cause for thankful happiness. So we do our duty, strive to help those who bear burdens, and thus we do surely lighten and forget our own. And thus may it ever be while life lasts, from this till our final temporal Saturday Night.

XVII.

Rest for the Weary.

HOW slow the hands creep over the dial; how the brain burns and throbs as we work and wait for the coming hour which will release us from labor! Life is but a trial—a sentence—an imprisonment for those who toil; and were it not that the Angel of Saturday Night, like some heaven-sent fairy, comes each week to release us from over-taxing work and lead us to rest with the loved ones, death would be sweeter than life, even without its golden rewards for those who try to be good and noble.

To-night we are too worn and weary to write as we would like. We are like thousands who, all the week, have toiled beyond their strength to earn comforts for the dear ones, and who now feel to envy those who sleep behind marble head-boards in the "silent city." Oh! for the good time coming, when we can be with the ones who wait our coming, and whose smiles are ever more life-giving than spring. The hours seem long as we watch the dial face, for the welcome that awaits us has in it that love which lures us to the happy eternal by mellowing the heart, purifying the soul, and giving us confidence in each other.

Sometimes we think life is not worth the living. It is not, to many. It would not be for any of us but for the unspoken beautiful which draws us captive to the hearth and fender. As love comes to us, so we give in return, each to each, with accumulative interest. Smiles are born of happy hearts. Happy hearts are born of better natures. Smiles brighten our pathway; and when the dearest eyes in all the world look into ours, so full, strong, deep and earnest, we could, should, and would dare any danger, face any death, or wrestle with any fate which stood between us and the only earthly reward there is to life!

We are weary, but only of toil. Others are weary. Strong men are trembling in their muscle to-night, for they have battled severely all the week to keep want and hunger from the sacred circle where gather those whose hearts, day by day, run more and more into each other. Young men, with hearts full of embryo happiness, golden dreams, in which warm lips, love-lit eyes, trusting hearts, and future homes of their own are mixed floating, as incentives to strive with earnestness — they are weary.

But the day comes when they will be more so, when they will go slowly to their homes with bent forms, as do thousands who will rest in their graves before there comes to any of us another Saturday Night.

And the watcher by the hearth is weary! She, too, has toiled all the week. That clean floor, that well-kept hearth and fender, the snowy linen, the clean dishes, the sweet, clean shelves in pantry and cupboard, the clean doors, walls, and windows; that look of home cheer which should mark every earthly heaven; that tidy, sweet, lovable look, no matter for the years, tell that she too has labored and is weary. Then, good man, working-man and brother in toil, be kind, speak kindly, act kindly, lovingly, to the one who has worked for you as you have for her.

She is the one who cares most for you, who in heart is the dearest; she is to you as you are to her — two silken strands weaving together to bless or to curse as you will. The world cares not for you. Not one of us is of account to the world, for it moves whether we do or not; it was here when we came; it will be here with all its cold, selfish indifference when we die, and centuries after we are forgotten except in the deeds we do worth remembering. After a time will come the final Saturday Night to all of us, and the only ones who will weep and mourn, as we would for them, will be the ones who welcome us to the hearth and fender; who love us far more dearly than pen or words of ours can tell; who have often been weary, but always entitled to more rest and happiness than any of us here below.

Let us love best those who are dearest and kindest, and most in sympathy. Very soon there will be no going forth Monday morning — no more use for the little tin pail — no more need to walk with rapid steps lest we be late. Instead of listening to the noise outside, of looking closely with eye and brain upon the work to do; instead of toiling for those we love and for ourselves, there will be a little room, with perhaps a few pictures therein — a weary watching of shadows on the wall — a nervous, tiresome, restless, turning upon a sick bed as we toss like infants, helpless in the care of the loved ones.

Then the hours will fly, oh! so swiftly, as we are called to look with eyes of life upon those who are left behind to weep, and pray, and mourn. Then will, like panoramas, pass by the work we have done, the plans made, and the results accomplished; the streets of the city, with their staring and glaring walls will fade out; the changing scenes of earth will melt out and float down the turbid waters of the past, the only pictures engraven upon our hearts being the faces, the forms, the smiles, the eye-whispers of the loved ones we hope soon to meet; and the only credentials for His beautiful land and a home where none but loved ones enter the good acts, kind words, and noble deeds, great or small, given by us to the ones who with us are ever weary but ever needing the love and kindness we who are strong at times fail to give.

When this day comes there will be no more weariness, while the prayers of those who will mourn our departure will bear us to the land of the leal, where we can rest, or return in spirit to guard and bless those dear to us now.

Life is nothing; but for those we love it would not be worth the living. Then let us all who are men, be better, truer, more deserving. Let us take more care of ourselves, of our health of our earnings, that those who look with joy for our coming may be glad, and by faith, love, kindness deserved, and trusting sympathy, help us all to reach the Eternal Island of the true, where there will be no more labor; no more oppression for poor; no more robbing of those who toil for the benefit of those who do not; no no more vain watchings, and no more Saturday Nights.

XVIII.

Only a Poor Old Wood-sawyer!

SATURDAY NIGHT, and the welcome rest it brings! And life spared, we hope, for some good purpose, as time will tell when the string of seven-day beads are all counted!

. . . . .

He could not have been less than seventy

years of age. We saw him this afternoon, with his ragged clothes, wrinkled face, bent form, and thin, white hair, working on the sidewalk, sawing a little, pine kindling-wood, and throwing it into the cellar, through a little round trap-hole. His battered hat was on a step hard by. His little old saw hardly felt the power that sent it slowly through the wood, for the arm was feeble, as was the life-current of the poor old man.

We paused in our walk to look at him. Time was cutting away at him as he was at the wood, and soon he too will drop out of sight. God give him good rest when comes the day.

"Good evening, uncle!"

"Eh-*cee!* ch-*cee!* eh-*cee!* eh-*cee!* ch-*cee!*"

He did not stop till the stick was in two, and we spoke in louder tone,—

"Good evening, uncle.. Your job is most done!"

He slowly raised from his labor, rubbed the bare right arm across his forehead, looked at us for half a minute, and slowly said,—

"Yes; my work *is* most done!"

"Let us saw a few sticks, just for luck and old times."

The old man looked at us from head to foot, shook his head, and said,—

"Please don't fool with an old man!"

"Let me take your saw."

Mechanically he handed it to us, and we finished his task while he sat and rested, evidently wondering if the "new man" at the job were crazy or a myth. And we thought, as we sawed the dozen sticks, that the work of the old-man *was almost done,* and wondered if God would doom us to live so long here, away from the beautiful "over there"! And we thought; and thought that man was much like the saw: went up and down, cutting his way through life, at last to get through just in time to see the sticks he has sawed taken for use by others!

Then, what do we amount to more than the saw? This! there is a power, a Grand Arm, that directs us for a purpose; that causes us to cut blocks, to shorten old styles of doing work, to fit our work to the great temple being built silently in the East.

Then we sat and talked a few moments with the old man. And he told us the simple story of a life — the first time he had ever told it. No romance, but plain truth. And this it was:

Born. Reared by wealthy parents near Rochester. Came to New York, years ago, when a young man. Clerk in a hardware store on lower Pearl Street. Gay fellow with the boys. Married. Spent his wife's fortune; buried her, lived in dissipation; "luck" went against him when his old cronies saw him going ruinward. Ten years he had lived in cellars and garrets, on floors, straw mattrasses, coarse food, and sometimes none, and sometimes good meals, as those for whom he had done odd jobs at times called him into the kitchen.

This was the story. Hardly more words than years to his life. But he was almost through work. A little longer, and then good-bye, old saw and weary tramps for a little work. He said the saw was better than none. "When I file the saw it works well. But men don't do so: sometimes they don't do anything for what you do for them!" This is what the old man said, and it struck us as a great truth sawed out of life by nearly eighty years of toil!

Then we walked and talked. The heart of the old man had gone. No home; not one to love or care for him. What mattered houses or lands to him; or horses or carriages; or diamonds, or jewelry? No one was glad when he came or sorry when he went. The joyous echoes of the past were drowned so deep in the dissipation of years agone, they came to him only in dreams!

What an ending to life! God's gift toward advancement frittered away! Thrown away, despised, trodden under feet, ignored, drowned in dissipation and murdered, while "good fellows" clanked glasses and laughed at the fools who raved of life, of love, of honor, of manhood, of earnings, that when came the day to rest, there might be a place. Even birds save bits of down and lint, carrying them miles to soften their nests!

And we came home, thinking of life and its duties, and of the poor old men all over the land. Of those who had no regard for the future when they dulled their lives foolishly and tossed the days down their throats. And of the poor old men, in shops, and on farms; and working by the roadside to catch up in the race, and to help bury in paupers' graves those still poorer than themselves. And of the poor old men whose nights are full of tremors and ugly dreams, as they sleep on the briars and thorns of that life from which they cut out the beautiful to save the bad!

What would you, honest reader, say to a man who should go into his flower-garden, and, with knife, shears, pincers, fingers, or hot poison, cut off, tear out, and kill the beautiful buds, flowers, and seeds; leaving the roots, sharp-pointed limbs, and odorless sticks as ornaments? Well, that man lives on each side of us. He lives everywhere. And when he dies, what a bouquet will his garden afford for the coffin! And there are girls — women, who thus do. God pity them, for they are insane!

And there are others who go into their garden, cutting out the roots that give troubles and against which toes are caught, and branches, that bear no flowers, and flowers that give no fragrant odor. Some will ride or walk by, and sneer at the honest worker to-day; but they pause to admire to-morrow! And they want to know how he made his garden so beautiful! And they will send there for flowers to deck the bridal vail or the funeral pall.

The poor old man passed on to his garret on Eighty-first Street, and we to our writing. Such poor old men we pity. No one seems to care for them. They are taxed on their matches, on their rags, on their crust of bread, on their pipe and tobacco, on their medicine to benefit the rich. And it must be so lonely, this being near the wharf, with no one to go ashore with you that you know, or who cares for you!

Give us years that bend the chin to the chest if you will, but, O God in Heaven, give us some one to love even then, when the night is coming upon us! The night that but hides the morn; but still, the night! It must be fearful to die alone—and no one so alone as the poor who are alone and unloved.

Kings and queens are those without dollars or dimes who may be old and poor, but yet loved and honorable. Hand in hand down the narrowing lane! There is glory in the old love, life in the old caresses, heart in the old kisses, and heaven in the flickering of that old life, which, with loved ones, wanders in beautiful gardens, from which those who wander and rest 'neath fragrant shades picked and clipped the thorns and brambles long ago.

Let us all speak kindly to those who are old and growing old. Very soon the narrowing road will shut them out, and very soon we, too, will go out. And as we do by the poor and aged ones, so will others do kindly or unkindly by us, when our work is ended and comes, to rich and poor, old and young, loved and unloved, the final Saturday Night.

XIX.

HOME TO THE LOVED ONES.

ALL the week at work. Day after day came and went like echoes from wondrous shores. Morn, noon, and night, in each other's hand, closed upon the labors of us all, and made another volume of seven good, bad, or indifferent chapters.

The work of the week is finished, and now,

weary, heart sore, doubting life and not fearing death, we put by the pen and go home with those who, with us, have labored hard all the week past.

Saturday Night is the jewel of His evening crown. It is the oasis on the desert of labor, for here we rest. A week is not much, yet it is more than a life to many. Look about.

See the honest laborers, the men of toil, the ones who are building up the country and working themselves into the graves for the benefit of others, or to sustain life. We have seen them all the past week — all the past weeks of life. Men in shops, in stores, in offices; men through whose veins the hot life of blood courses as they build castles in the air for themselves and their loved ones to occupy; men who have long since passed the centre, and now verge upon the eternal. All the days we have thought of the workingmen, of the ones who are, by labor, either of head or hand, supporting themselves and home ones.

To-night they are going home. Tired, and needing rest, nervous, and needing kind words, they are going to their loved ones, and most earnestly do we say, joy, love, peace, and happiness be theirs. For the workingmen deserve all this.

And, good wife, when he comes home tired, be kind to him. Hours after hours, days after days, he works to make a home. He works for you and the little ones. He thinks of you often — so often! He saves where he might spend foolishly, and thinks of a thousand plans to benefit his loved ones and beautify his home.

See the books, the papers, the pictures, the carpets, the little keepsakes he has from time to time brought with him. Each article cost him toil. His hands may be hard, but his heart is warm. No man in all the world gives so liberally to help the needy and relieve distress as does the man who earns his bread in the sweat of his face, and by the muscle of his arms. It may be but little he gives, but that little is a part of himself—drops from the fountain which is filled but once, and which is lowered and lessened each week when comes Saturday Night.

Hour after hour we sit and think of the little homes of America. We look in upon thousands and thousands who see us not, and never think of our looking. We love the homes of those who labor, for they seem dearer than the homes of the rich, who need no one to pity them. We look in upon those who live in little rooms up stairs — small rooms in cellars. Upon those who have homes, whole homes of their own; we see, in some, good wives waiting, with cheerful face, the coming of the tired one who is so loved. And we see, in some, clean, happy children, joyful, for papa is soon coming to kiss, to romp, to gladden. Then we say, God bless the workingmen who have homes, no matter whether they like us or not.

And in some homes we see wives cross and peevish, dirty, slatternly, careless. They are not the girls once so loved, for time has wrought changes. And we see children, dirty and unrestrained, noisy and saucy, reflecting no credit on parents.

And we see homes where the floors are bare, the walls unornamented by a single picture, the cupboard empty, the coal-box empty or the wood pile low, the home ones clad in rags; for the one who should care for and protect them has spent his earnings in dissipation, to make attractive those places which ruin him. But we will not chide, for may be cold words, hot words, cutting words, and that unspoken and unspeakable sorrow of the heart which no one can find words to tell all of, has sent him often to any place rather than the cruel mockery of home. God pity all of us!

Do you ever think, working brother, of home and the beauties you can crowd therein? Loved ones, who are so happy when you come with kind words to greet them. Rooms made beautiful by result of labor; books, pictures, papers, magazines, in which you can read the thoughts of those who toil with the brain. And as you think of home all the week, are you not glad that there comes Saturday Night for us to give to those who have seen us so little all the week? We do not like cold homes, cheerless homes, where the heart is a tortured prisoner, but a bright, happy home, where the loved wait our coming.

The home we can have, if we will it; the home we can work for and be thankful for. The home where a warm, true, trusting heart, dearer almost than the promise of Heaven, waits our coming. The home where she waits, with bursting heart, deep love-lit eye, and moist, loving lips, to welcome us as, hand in hand, heart to heart, there is given such a welcome and unspoken vows for the future as no tongue or pen can tell. Home, where the heart is at rest, where one can sit for hours reading the volumes of love, unwritten, as they come from the eye that telegraphs to eye words and secrets others know not of.

Would to Him who gives out the new days and calls in the old ones, torn, blackened, disgraced and blotted by us on earth, that in all the land were none but happy homes, true loves and true hearts for all who toil, and bear burdens of heart or body. And if words of ours, or the energies of life, can or will make even one poor mortal happier or better; if words we can say which come from the heart can lighten the load all must bear, then will we be more than thankful that God gave us life and a heart to think of and write for those who, with us, have toiled all the week, and who would rest Saturday Night.

XX.

About that Little "Yes."

LAST Saturday Night a maid! This Saturday Night a wife!

We knew her years ago, when but a little girl; a romping, bright-eyed, pretty-faced little darling, the pet of all and the promise of surpassing loveliness. Year by year she grew, till the years came upon her like flakes of snow to protect her loving purity, and at last her heart warmed with a new love; and one Saturday Night the "Yes" she said, closed the past and opened the future to — God only knows what!

It was one night when the week was resting from its whirl, and the good angel was weeping over our records, as the revolving days had stamped the good and the bad of our lives on the lasting pages before him, that a chosen one came to the door. How her heart throbbed, as it trembled, for, it knew not what. The hours had been longer than their wont all day, for *he* was coming. The sunset seemed so long a-coming; the twilight seemed so loitersome, even after the golden pattern for the morrow's clouds had been left in the west, that a shade of anxiety rested over the face of the darling who waited.

But he came. Who could not tell his step from all others? And who touched the door knob as he? No one! And by her side he sat. Hand in hand, palm on palm resting, eye reading eye, and hearts sweetly communing. The hours of man were the seconds of God, so quickly did they drop into the well of time. And as the new week came, with its flowery promises to cover the sorrows of the old between the dead "now" and the living "then;" as the seven-day volume was closed, not lips alone, but hands, eyes, heart, and soul said, "Yes!"

One long, pure, trusting, lingering kiss, calling back all the kisses before given! and to the new week was born a new betrothal. This was then; one of the Saturday Nights of the past. And since then there was another kiss, as out on the great sea went the new voyagers, brave, trusting, hopeful, loving.

God be with them. And God be with her. She is good and pure. She has given him all of her past, present, and future, even to the foot of the beautiful throne. Her dreams in the past are on the shelves of the future; God grant they may blossom more beautiful than the budding.

But these words from a friend who loves those who love. From one who is hastening on to the shore which bids good-bye to every Saturday Night, and crosses us to the golden Sabbath of a more busy rest. Busier, for we shall have more to do; more rest, for we shall know how better! These words from one who has had joys and sadness, oh, so deep and wearisome to heart and brain:

The future of life is much as the past and the present. Not all the clouds we look upon are lined with that silver we can easily reach, though there is a lining for us if we but seek it aright. Not every flower on the distant plain to which we are walking is fragrant, nor the coloring as bright as in our dreams, for then we have glimpses of the beautiful Eternal Land to which the soul strays while we sleep.

There will come trials and sorrows, and troubles will ride on disappointments to find lodging in our hearts. But they will go as they come if we do not bid them to stay! There will be sad hours; for these we all have; even Christ, our Redeemer, had. But only for a time!

When comes the night, he will come, perhaps tired and weary, while you are rested. Be kind to him. Little do ye know of man's temptations. Thus it was from the first, and we shall be forgiven as we forgive others. Do not expect too much. Wooing is the blossom; wearing is the fruit, which lasts only with care! And as ye are hopeful, so will ye be happy. The new life is opening before you. The great mission must be filled, for thus is the vineyard worked from the beginning.

Oh the beauty of that faith which sets two hearts voyaging across the wondrous ocean. The journey may be long or short for one or both; but there is a meeting over there for those who loved on earth. The days go by like shadows in pursuit of dimmer ones. The reality comes to mock the ideal. The trials come to perfect our love and strengthen our faith in, and usefulness for the future.

All over the land are those who last Saturday Night were maidens, who now are wives. God bless all such. And may the married ones ever be mated. And if not, then let the heart speak, for the bird will rest and fold its wings where its home is, no matter how far away.

Let those who love, love more and be good to each other, for thus life rests easy on us. Keep back the cross words, and drive doubts of him or her from your hearts. Strive to be good and kind. Often sit together as before wedlock, which, as a ribbon or a chain, joined you together, were it before man or before Him who holds us all in keeping. Rest on the roses, not the thorns! Look over little evils, and great ones will not come so quickly! Bear with life's burdens bravely, and they will be lighter! Strive and to make others so. Guard well your hearts to be happy and your homes, beautifying both day after day.

Let no Saturday Night come that the one you love is not in heart dearer to you; let no new Sunday volume of days be opened till the errors of the last be told and forgiven; then will you be happy. And you, brothers, who toil, let no Saturday Night come that you do not add something to the comforts of home and the loved one; and the secret of happiness is before you.

God bless all who toil; who struggle; who sincerely love each other. Each of us has another heart to make happy; and from the lessons of the past let us all learn wisdom for the future.

But all are not happy; all cannot be. Hearts will wander to their resting; but when that rest is found let the door be closed, that none else enter; that we may, with the ones we truly love, in health or sickness, poverty or wealth, now as then, go hand in hand, by day and by night, in sunshine and in storm, hopeful and happy, with trusting hearts to that land where never comes a Saturday Night.

XXI.

She Brought a Skeleton.

SEVEN days more wound on the invisible reel! And each day a record for His inspection. If there is much we would like blotted out now, full of life and business that we are, how much is there for Him to shake His head at; how much we would wish had not been written by that wondrous pen when the record of life is open before us! Will we believe that record — those facts — when the book is passed to us, and there comes before us page after page, marking the days from birth to burial? Will we not think the record of some one else has been taken down by mistake? No? Will we believe when we *see?* Yes!

And who of us will have credits on that book O that all of us might have more than we shall have! and then there will be none too many But not of this to-night.

To-day we have been thinking. This morning there came to our private room a sad-faced woman, a stranger to us. A thousand miles and more had she ridden to tell us her simple yet sorrowful story, and to ask the advice of one she believed would advise honestly. The tears ran down her cheeks, like rain down window-panes when the storm is terrible outside, as hers was in.

She was a wife — a mother. She came to

show us the skeleton in her soul; to tell us her sorrow. Her only daughter, a fair girl of several teens, had gone from her. The cruel treatment of a father had driven the poor girl out upon the world. From home she went to honest labor; from this to companionship with those whose hearts and self-control are not anchored; from this to an assumed name and into the whirlpool of fast life in this terrible city.

Could we find her? Would we find her? Dare we find her? Could we save her? Would we, and how? And the tears came out to give her heart room for its sobs, its sighs, its sorrows, and its sadness!

Yes: we can find her, and we will; and some night like this we will tell you where, and what she said.

And we have been thinking all the day. Thinking of those who bear sorrows, and whose hearts are heavy as if laden with molten potash, which eats, and burns, and scars, beyond God's shown power to heal, this side the great well-making.

We see persons on the streets — in their homes. They toil, and rest, and laugh, and weep. There is a volcano in each heart, throwing out bitterness and sadness, yet the world knows not and cares not. Then why uncover a disfigured corpse for others to gaze on and satisfy morbid desires? Only to those who are friends!

We have been thinking of the thousands of beautiful girls, who are lost to their homes and themselves, flying like down before the gale, or in the draft which draws them to certain heat, blackness, and destruction. The dress is not more varied than their adopted names. And how many of these are wept for by mothers who mourn as only mothers can mourn, and are cursed as only men can curse? They who are thus fading before perdition's fires are not happy, for there is no happiness out of that path of velvet sward hedged by the beautiful flowers of Right.

Did you ever see swamps covered with a seeming carpet of beautiful green? And did you ever see men and cattle *wading* and sinking where all, from even a short distance, seemed so fair?

There are many swamps, as God duplicates His creation.

The one who wept before us this morning had been remiss in her duty. She paid the interest of her penalty in sobs and tears; death alone can pay the principal!

Mothers — fathers, — think of your daughters. Love them more; care for them; protect them; guard them more closely. The dress you make to-day is worn for a long journey! The little one in the cradle, or playing at your feet, you watch or neglect in her plays or romps, will be a curse or a blessing as her early education is right or wrong.

Some there are, born to be bad, but they are few. God will never ask for our dollars, but will demand the souls we save or lose — which He gave.

There are wives and mothers, in thousands and tens of thousands of homes where this chapter will be read. God bless all who read it, and all who do not. And there are wives and mothers in the grasp of poverty, but not so poor as the one who came to us this morning, for her *wealth* had gone, perhaps never to be returned, at least with seal unbroken and stamp of purity uncancelled!

There are those in little cabins, log-houses rented rooms, garrets, cellars, farm houses, village homes, city residences; those who toil on plain or prairie, on hillside and in the valley; who are poor, but not so poor as the broken-hearted mother who came to us for help to-day.

Perhaps you toil and mourn for the dead; but that is not dying for the living! There are those of women who rise early, prepare the morning meal, rub, work, scrub, make, mend and labor, days and months; who may have rough, coarse, brutal husbands, who only marry to gratify passion and have a target to fire their anger at; wives who are neglected, uncared for, deceived, betrayed; who are compelled by that society which sanctions legalized and solemnized prostitution to take to their arms and bosoms those they once swore to love, warm from the passionate embrace of other loves; who envy the rich and mourn over their lot, yet who are rich compared to the mother who came to say she had lost her treasure.

Have you a young husband who loves you, who is true to you? Then love him, no matter how close the wolf stands to your door. Have you a husband who smiles on you, who is kind, and good, and earnest, and manly, and true-hearted, yet who is not so rich, or so gay, or so smart as the husband of some other woman?

Then love him, and help him, and each add, by gentle touch, sweet caress, and ready care, to happiness. Have you a *friend* who is good, and kind, and devoted, and all in all to you as you are to him or her? Then continue so till comes the mating, and be happy, for the little cares which annoy, bother, worry, and trouble you, are nothing compared to the skeletons which burden the souls of thousands who would be happy if laden with no more care and sorrow than you are laden with.

And have you work to do, a living to earn, a destiny to fill? Then do it as 'twas given you; bear up as well as you can; think how many are more miserable than you are, and if you have little ones, — have daughters to love and care for, — teach them aright and thank God that the heart treasures you would take *over the river* with you are not, by your neglect, carelessness, or negligence, lost overboard as food for the sharks which so thickly infest life's sea. And teach your sons to be good, honorable, upright; to be men with pluck enough to defend those who are innocent, that they may not, from lack of protection, give and partake of other dishes than those flavored by love and restrained by reason. Then will we all be better and the less to give us sorrow when comes to the week, or to the life, Saturday Night.

XXII.

Going Home.

IS *it not grand?*

Another Saturday Night—seven leagues nearer *home*—seven links nearer heaven—seven of His steps nearer the throne of love eternal; most wondrous, grand, and beautiful. Is it not grand? This idea of death. Not death, for there is no death! But the sleeping here to waken there to the new and the eternal when there will be no more weary struggling, relying so much on our own efforts; but lines and lights, duties and occupations clearly defined. On being brought to light we shall see glories in the East, shall be advanced to the Most High for instructions and rewards, and then shall know something of the wonderful so many dread to reach.

Death!

Life!

And life eternal! Is it not grand to contemplate the calling home and the removing of that which prevents our seeing into or of the future? So-called death is nothing. We lay aside the garb of labor, the soiled garments worn to protect our bodies from the dirt of the shop, and bid the week " good-bye," to enter upon the Sabbath—eternal rest. Who regrets bidding his shopmates or fellow-laborers " good-night" when the work of the week is ended and he can throw off the dirty apron and go to meet his treasures — the loved ones, who wait his coming as he will wait the coming of others?

We take shopmates and fellow-laborers we love home with us to be with them while we rest. So shall we take our loved ones, that is, our dearly loved ones, home with us to the Eternal Gardens, where the flowers that bloom are our good deeds, planted on earth to blossom in Heaven. And who of us have planted? Who of us are planting? Who of us dare plant — have pluck to do right and plant for eternity?

Who would walk the Eternal Gardens and see others resting under the shades, enjoying the delicious perfumes of good deeds done on earth, themselves with never a tree or flower to show?

Then we shall see the glories and the mysteries of the hereafter; shall be with the loved ones who wait our coming; shall see and know the infinite Power to whom our prayers have been made; shall, perhaps, know of the wondrous plans of Him who is so far above us, and rest as does the infant on its mother's breast, its Heaven, happy beyond words in having reached the gardens of God, rather than being lost in the wilderness outside His beautiful realms.

With Him will dwell those who love Him; not the cold and rotten of heart, who claim qualities they possess not. With Him will be those who have faith, hope, love,—a part of God himself,—in their hearts; those who dare to, and try to do right by all; who have hearts that ache, and eyes that weep for the woes of others.

Those who dread death are those who do not deserve it; those who deserve no release from the cares, trials, struggles, betrayals and disappointments of this which we call, but which is not, life. This "waiting-room," filled with those who know us not, who tread us down to rush past and over us, is not Home. We are simply passengers, waiting here in the smoke, dirt, dust, profanity, and wickedness of life for the arrival of the coach which is to take us Home! And *there* we shall find our friends, and generous welcome. Those who are going to their loved ones are happy. Those who are going to prison, and who go they know not where, go simply because they can no longer stay. God pity them, for they need pity!

The only thing is this: What will they say of us when others fill our places? What will those who join in, look at, or hear of our funeral and burial say? Will we be missed, or will our going be like the wind which passes, is gone, and no one cares whither? God grant that they say of us all more of good than they are called to forget and forgive of the bad. And may we, when going home, leave no memory of wrong, of neglect, of sharp, bitter words, of unkindness, or good deeds we might have done, omitted; for after we have *gone home* there will be no returning,—no renewal of labor or another week to improve on or correct the errors of this. Give us all hearts to do right; to speak well of those we know not of, or know to be good. Give us, who have opportunities to do good, a heart to heed and an eye to see wherein our duty and our true happiness lies, that dying or *going home*, our thoughts may be of love and faith rather than of dread and soul-piercing regrets.

Little by little, we mount upward, step after step. Little by little we win victories; here a triumph, there another. Little by little we win love, and prove our manhood. Little by little we earn and build around us till the waste becomes fertile, the new home an old one, the cabin a cottage, the cottage a home, where are our earthly treasures of the heart. Working-man and brother, do you think? Waiting wife, toiling mother or hopeful betrothed, little by little your words mellow the heart and win him to you. Working boy, who now bends to poverty's burden as we have so oft, in the years agone, little by little the shadows come upon us, the flowers bloom, the fruit ripens, the earnest endeavor wins success, and you mount to the higher plane of true manhood, as you are true, earnest, honest, industrious, and deserving of love, of fame, or position, as all who labor are deserving rest and reward when comes Saturday Night.

XXIII.

Soliloquy of a Happy Man.

IN the prime of life and happy as the day is long. How few there are who can say as much. Those who cannot I pity. I envy no man, for I am happy. I have health and am contented. It is true I own no palace, no carriage; no great wealth to bother me, and annoy with unceasing care; yet I am very happy for all.

I have worked like a man. When I could not do better I was content with doing well. When I had health I preserved it, and when in need of money earned it. While others dissipated I rested, and gained strength for the cares, duties, and labors of the morrow.

The days came, some bright and some cloudy; but they were no worse to me than others, nor were all the beauties for me alone. I did not expect too much; then I was not disappointed. The weeks came and went, but did not rob me of my manhood. I spent no hours in repining. Throwing dirt against a window you cannot see through will not remedy the defect of vision, or make the view more clear.

I have a home, and some one to love me as I do her. And my home is the happiest in all the world. We try to make it so. She and I try, and we never weary. Years ago I told her I loved her. And I did love her. And she loved me. Our years were fewer than now. When we plighted troth, and when we knelt before the altar, I took her to my heart, as she took me to hers. And I have tried to be good. When I did not wish to fall or stumble, I kept away from temptation, and thus lost all desire to walk in dangerous places. Being a man, it was my duty to provide a home and strive to adorn it. Little by little, as I gained the means, have I done so, till, from the desert of life, has sprung a loved place of rest, and here we live in, by, and for each other.

Sometimes little clouds come up; but we look not upon them and they soon go. Sometimes I am sick, tired, weary. Then she loves me even more tenderly, holds my aching head to her heart, presses the hair back from my brow, kisses me so sweetly! and my troubles sink into the fading fog of the past under her loving, caressing, and gentle touch. She whom I love is very, very good to me, and I could not be otherwise to her and be a man.

We share our joys and sorrows. We strive to please each other, and pay little attention to the words of others, and thus secure happiness. And when she is tired and sick, then it makes my heart large to help her, to pet her, to love and care for her. Then her heart is at rest, her mind at ease; she says the look of my eyes is more than medicine, and the gentle touch of love more than all the world for her restoration.

We are not ashamed to love each other. This we promised. We are not ashamed if others know it. God keep our hearts thus mated, and who shall say "nay"? We live for each other. We live in the house we live in, and not in the one across the way! We are happy because we strive to be. We love each other because we have so promised. We care for each other, for thus is that love which grows and blesses us watered and invigorated. I want none of that which is forbidden, for it brings no good or happiness, and I'd rather keep unsullied the manhood which wins and retains the love of the pure, loving, trusting heart I am so happy in keeping.

And days I work for her — for us — for our home. And nights I rest. We sit by the same fire, quaff from the same cup, read by the same light, read each other's eyes; and when that irresistible impulse calls lip to lip, and heart to heart, not for the wealth of kings or greatness of empires would I give up or forsake the bower where our love is undisturbed, no matter at whose coming.

Yes, I am happy. We are happy. Our house is but small, but our hearts are large. She never speaks cross to me, nor I to her. At times when I write there comes behind me a soft footstep; I feel the presence of a loved one; I close my eyes to receive a gentle kiss on my forehead; an arm steals around my neck; as I turn my head eyes that tell so much meet mine; our lips meet; she sits on a low chair, with head resting on my lap; my writing is only interrupted as I bend over at times to kiss the eyes and lips of her who is resting, and we are very, very happy. And sometimes, when I am tired and weary, it is my head that rests in her lap. She works and talks to me, or reads while I toy with her hand, listen, half dreamingly, to her voice, and wonder how many years God will give us thus to love each other on earth before we are called home. Then we talk of the past, the present, and the future. And we, while thus resting, unreel the ribbon of the past to find but few spots other than of beauty thereon. And when we find such a spot, we write "repentance" across it, that when God sees it He may know we have suffered and sorrowed and tried to atone for the making it. Then we feel happier. Then we rest sweeter in each other's hearts, and for fear I may die and leave her to battle on alone, I plan to-day and work to-morrow for her protection after I am gone, if it is for me to prepare a place for her in the eternal land.

Perhaps you do not like this, my writing, but I do not care. We are happy. Even now her head rests under my left hand, and since the first word of this paragraph my lips have rested on hers. And we find our happiness in pleasing each other, and with this happiness comes strength to do what others fail in.

And when comes the hour for labor on the morrow, we shall there be found. And such duties as the day may bring we will be ready for. And we'll try each to do our duty well. And when comes the morrow night, at home will we rest, for this is the secret of happiness. Others may dissipate and wander for the bitter-sweet; we are content to live as God intended. And we are not envious, for in time will come the luxuries of life, but they will not add to our happiness.

Yes, I am happy; for I try to be. I strive to live for some good. I use only kind words. I try to benefit others, and have the manhood to do that which I deem a duty. And this course brings and retains the respect of the good. It gives me the love and confidence of my friends; and those who are not, it is not worth while to strive to please. And as I am happy, so can others be if they will, even if they are, like me, simple laborers, taking care to avoid paths which lead to temptation, and not afraid or ashamed to be men for the preservation of that manhood which no poverty can wrest from us, if we respect ourselves, and which gives us strength to work the days of the week, and a relish for rest, with work well done, when comes the Saturday Night.

XXIV.

Very Lonely.

ONCE more! Another Saturday Night! Again has the raven borne its load of seven bundles back to the shelves of the past, to be entombed till the final settling! Another weekly volume bound and laid away,— each of the seven chapters the book contains sealed forever. No matter how many blots or wrong figures, we cannot open the volume to erase or change — the record is complete so far.

Our past is His present! It is His safe wherein is locked, beyond the reach of our opening or genius of our keys, life records to be looked at whenever He wills. And He calls us to settlement, whether we are ready or no. Oh! that none but good records were against all of us!

But no more of this to-night. It is not of the past, and yet it is. All the week we have toiled with brain and hand, till head and body be weary. But now we can rest, and lift from the cooling spring of memory beadlets strung with pearl drops, wherein and whereon are beautiful pictures. We see a thousand faces thus. Faces of those who little think we see them. We hear the laugh, the voices of friends, as we shape the pearls thus drawn out together; we feel the earnest grasp of heart-warmed hands, and live over again the years that are lost, as a traveller would retrace his steps, and stop only at the most beautiful places he visited in the years afled.

And as we look these scenes over, we feel lonely to-night. No one in the room save ourself and the unseen spirits which fill the air, and which come and go at our heart-stilled bidding. The white dial of the watch before us seems to-night so much like a face we know: often have our eyes rested thereon. We listen to the "*think-quick — think-quick*" of the heart-work of this little mechanism, and cannot half think.

. . . .

All gone!

The loved guests we had with us have gone. There were spirits of those who have crossed the river before us, — and the spirits of those who to-night are dreaming. For do you not know that when we sleep our souls journey. Sometimes to lands we know not of as we live. Sometimes to greet spirits over yonder! Sometimes wandering with spirits from over there! And sometimes we wander among old scenes known before we became of earth, as in the future state we will roam the aisles of the past, which is our present. When we sleep, school is out, and spirits play! And sometimes we sleep while awake,—and start, we know not why! It is only the spirit—the soul, which has been playing truant, visiting miles away—*returned to its penance!*

When the old house is worn out we move into another one! And this is all there is of death. And were it not that all we love cannot go at the same time with us to the new home, we would not care how quick the old house might fall.

. . . At times we feel sad and lonely.

Waves run not smooth like placid water, nor does life. It may "over yonder," and this is our hope, *our full faith.*

But to-night we miss somebody. Our thoughts are with some one else. The room seems very still. Never so still before. We long to *be there,*— to be away from here; to look into certain eyes adown whose depths are traced characters others cannot, but which we can read. We would feel the soft, sweet breath of some one; we wait the pen for a hand to touch ours, for loved fingers to rest as before on our almost bursting temples; but alas! the eyes are not before us only as they glide with the pen point across the paper on which we write! And the dear fingers will not still the throbs which pain us. The sweet lips we have so often pressed the very soul upon and into will not come to us to-night, nor can we feel the throbbing of that heart wherein we know our image is enshrined as an emerald is surrounded by diamonds pure and of wonderous lustre.

Did you ever wish *somebody* with you when miles were holding hands, not hearts, apart? Did you who read these lines ever feel *so hungry* because *some one* more than loved was not with you? Did you ever pace the floor, press against the pane, listen to footsteps, grow heartsick over an absent one, till it seemed as if you must go somewhere, anywhere? Did you ever grow faint and weary of life in knowing that *somebody*, no matter who, were away, and you just dying for their presence?

When the work of the day is ended, then we want rest. Not alone the easy chair, the yielding sofa; not one of your hard, stiff, quakerish contrivances, but a comfort; not alone the carpeted floor and pictured walls,— that which gives rest to eye and body,— but we want rest for the heart. Basking in the sunshine of love. Loved lips, speaking eyes, gentle hands, kind words, generous kisses given by pure, sweet, unstained, unpolluted lips. This is rest. To know that *some one*, no matter who,— and yet it does matter,— is with you, by you, of you, for you, to you, pure, good, loving, gentle-hearted, is the heaven of this life, as God is of the next.

But to-night we are alone; yet not alone. The words she said, the kisses she gave us, the caresses none can rob us of; the plans, and hopes, and promises, and darings of and confidence in the future,— all these are with us. Like gauze over choice paintings, so does her love keep from us that which mars and weakens.

Pretty soon! Before many days or weeks! We shall meet again. Very soon in dreams. We will find her when the body is at rest. We will not be lonely then, for long before morning we will be more than a hundred leagues away, and whither we go we will not tell!

And some day!

Thank God for that! Then we who work can rest. If we save we shall enjoy! If we are good we shall be happy; that is, happier than if we are not. And we can work for others, can speak kind words for those who toil, and suffer, and sorrow, and hope, and wait, and with brave, patient, trusting hearts, sit on the shore of the inrolling sea, waiting for the golden ship and the calm which settles on the waves to still them. God bless those we love, all whom we work for, and keep all from the perils of this and every Saturday Night.

XXV.

About Our Neighbor.

SATURDAY NIGHT of last week our neighbor lived beside us, in a little home all his own. We have chatted with him by the hour. Where he came from we do not know. He was a good fellow; we liked him, and never thought to ask where he came from. When came Saturday

Night, he would come to our little study and talk with us, sometimes half an hour.

Then he would go home to his dear ones of the heart, and love them, and kiss them, and pet them, and romp with them. His wife always seemed so happy; her eyes, dark and beautiful, ran over with love, and when his name was mentioned, would sparkle as her heart danced to the joyful tune, "My darling is he, and all mine own."

Sometimes we could hear them reading to each other. Once we saw him reading by her side as she sat rocking to sleep a dear little one in her arms. He read from a book, and as he read one hand rested carelessly, but speaking volumes, on one of hers, inspiring him with the good. Then we saw through the broken blind, as we stood against the fence watching, that she stopped her rocking, looked tenderly upon the face of her sleeping babe, and then upon the loved and manly form beside her. Their eyes met. He closed the book, and drew his chair still nearer — rested his head on her bosom beside the face of the little sleeper, with his face upturned. She looked upon her treasures a moment; a tear fell from her eyes; their lips met and drank from the luscious joy and happy fulness of the heart.

They were happy; and we mused in our room an hour, disturbed at last by the walk of a drunken man going to his home.

Ours was a good neighbor. He minded his own business. He spoke but kind words. He worked in a blacksmith-shop. His hands were very hard, and his muscles! How we envied him this overplus of strength. What he had he earned, and what he earned he saved to beautify his home. He was not stingy nor miserly. He gave dimes to poor children, and was for his little ones a God-given plaything, dearer to them than all the toys in the world. He left his care in the shop; took his heart home, hung his dignity with his coat on a hook, and lived for the ones he loved. And that is the way to live. Why bother to please those who care not for you?

. . . .

This Saturday our neighbor moved away. We knew he was intending to go soon. He told us months ago that a man was building a new house and a better one for him over the river, on a neat, clean, wide street! He said he was going there to live, and to earn better wages in another shop. And he said his loved ones would be nearer. We told him, years ago, if he wanted a better place to work in, and a better house to live in, and better times generally, it lay in his power to obtain them. And he worked, and saved, and kept his manhood pure and unweakened by excess or dissipation. He wanted to have a better home, and he saved his earnings till at last he could have a better one.

We don't know as yet where it is, but are to go over the river in a few days and will find him. We have the directions. We know who he went to work for. A very liberal employer, who employs none but the best and most deserving workmen! And His work is always perfect. We know where to find our neighbor when we go over there, and shall be glad to meet him. A wagon came and took him away. And it took all he had ever earned. The good man sent the wagon, but we did not know who drove it.

It is a little lonesome now, for our neighbor has moved. We look at the little worn-out house he left, and look ahead with joy to the time when we shall leave our little house for a better one over where he has gone. We know where he has gone, for all these years he has been wishing to be there — to better himself when he moved; and as he has laid up something and proved himself a good workman, he would not go into a poorer house, or work for a poorer employer than he had on this side the river.

This house where our neighbor lived is empty. It is to be torn down in a few weeks, and the material all carried away. But our neighbor has gone to a better house, for he was a good and a deserving man.

. . . .

Our neighbor has gone!

We did not see him go. But to-day we saw a span of horses drawing his house away! His house was in a long affair used for moving such houses. It was moved away for the reason that our neighbor had got through with it — gone to his beautiful home over the river, where the smiles of God tint the flowers of the eternal, and where all is love, kindness, and that perfection unknown here.

We shall not weep over the house our neighbor — our good friend — moved from, for that will do no good. To be sure, it is lonesome without him, but we know where to find him. The other day a man moved away, but we know not where he went to. He had no steady employment when he lived by us. He worked for almost any one, but he was not a good workman, and could find no employment *over there!* He worked mostly for himself, and people took but little interest in him. He had some friends, but they lived all about in bad places, and we think he has gone to find them. We are sorry we did not go over the river, but cannot help it.

And before long we shall go to meet our friend. And he will introduce us to the other workmen, and indorse us; and we shall all be friends at once, and be with those who are there paid hourly and not compelled to wait till the coming of Saturday Night.

XXVI.

Plain Words to Those we Love about our Home.

WE made it.

A home. Not a palace full of unused rooms, strange echoes, deserted chambers, hollow sounds, musty smells, and horrible-patterned carpets; but a neat, cosy home, where we live every day, happy in what we have, envious of no one, caring for our real wants, and giving no hospitality to imaginary ones.

A few years since we began without a dollar. One night our palms rested in each other, our lips met as never before, we promised earnestly and faithfully; have kept vows deeply graven on our hearts.

Then we started out on the voyage of united love. The great sea sang murmuring at our feet. Its distance was flecked with tiny sails. There were icebergs and green isles in the distance, but none near the velvet shores! Is it thus to tempt people? So or not so, those who look beyond the reach of momentary vision can see open sailing,—that icebergs can be missed and the green isles far out yonder be reached.

But not except those who sail the craft be of one mind! Let both steer for the same port and channel: it will be reached. But, alas! too many sail on, wrapped only in the present squandering of the future, and soon put back for another craft or float on the surf that throws and dashes and spatters itself in mockery over the rock-ribbed shore, not harder than the composite of error on which many a frail bark is stranded.

There is much in mating. There is much more in not overloading the craft. There is much in not taking too many passengers with you; and there is much in working the ship together, and very much in not giving to others the delicacies which never outlast the voyage except used only by those who put them up for their own use!

But no more of the sea: we must not float
So far from the Shore—
So far from our Home—
So far from our Love—
So far from our Duty—
So far from our Happiness—
So far from Ourselves!

 . . . .

How did we win this home?

Little by little. Thanking God for yesterday, for *to-day*, for to-morrow; for hope and for pluck. It did seem hard to begin from nothing years ago, but we thus begun. We decided to fit our craft for a long voyage, in hope to visit very many of the distant isles. So we saved. What was earned by the plow, the spade, the scythe, the axe, the pick, the labor of hands, was saved; not to be hoarded, but to be spent.

The money earned in the shop by the forge fire did not float off in steam like the water put on burning coal; it did not thin off into shavings fit only to kindle desires; it did not drop into the pile of cloth scraps, leather bits, and waxed ends; we did not leave it fastened to the cup of dissipation, nor invest it in weeds to grow up and choke our manhood.

It was saved for the good it might do; was paid to those who built our home, and those who in a thousand other places were working to make this and that of the useful and beautiful, to be purchased, paid for, and enjoyed by all who would or will make home attractive.

Is it not wonderful how working-men help each other? And how little we do for those who made all these beautiful things for us!— these carpets, chairs, tables, pictures, glass, and frames; the house we live in, the stove we cook upon, the bed we sleep on, the food we eat, the clothes we wear, the dishes we use, the medicines we take, the piano we listen to, the jewelry our loved wears, the books and papers we read; the pen we use, the ink we are wasting, the watch which tells us of the hour, the curtains which exclude the glance of eyes outside as we sit writing, stopping only to pet, and kiss, and love the dearest one on earth,—who says she cannot help loving us!

Why! If all the men and women, boys and girls, who had worked on the articles in our home should call to-night; who would—who could care for our guests? They would be here by the thousand! Verily, the idea, the truth of our own littleness, as we have to think of how little account we are to others, and how many others work for us, is enough to drown the soul into its own shrinkage!

But it is not of this—but our home.

When night comes, here we rest to gather strength and grow heart-mellow in love. Here we have a castle a king might envy, all won by honest toil. The rooms are always so neat and in order. The bedclothes clean, the sweeter to rest for the better health for the morrow. We have not so much as one cross word in all the year. We care not what others say of us, for the sun of happiness draws its warmth, not from what others say or do, but what we do or think of ourselves.

When our friends come they are very welcome. Little or much that we have, they are indeed welcome. We never fix up for anybody;

but keep fixed up, as good wives say, for ourselves. Then we are never surprised. If people come to see us they are welcome. If they come to feast on fat things, they can have no better than we have, without going to a hotel, — and then they may not. If we have a crust, and that only, half is theirs. We have no parlor for them alone, for it is all parlor in our home; all as nice as we can have it; we keep no room locked, darkened, musty, and unopened only at stated seasons, to show how foolish we are not to enjoy the good and comfort of life as we live, while waiting, as it were, for the hearse.

The best we have earned is none too good for our love, who is the best of all, and for her are all these purchased. We do not like to see people sit in the hot sun when a shade is close by, nor live in bare rooms in order to show people they do not know how to enjoy parlors. Empty parlors are but musty tortures: vain displays of taste used in too many instances only for weddings and funerals. Rightly kept, they are homes; securely locked up, they are prisons or sepulchres of ignored joys, comforts, and happiness.

Our home is our parlor. Our parlor is our home. We labor day after day. And as our will to dare, and power to accomplish, like the darkness, fades out before the coming of the great light, we strive for the goldening of our love, for the beautifying of our home for the great preparation. Those who care not for their homes here,—how can they care for them in the hereafter? The present is but the fitting of the future. As we strive here we are rewarded there. You need not tell us that we enter our new homes as we came here,— empty-handed or empty-hearted.

What did Christ say about the talent which was hidden in a napkin? Pause and look for the meaning of the simile.

All we earn, save, or gather here of the good, the pure, and the noble, is credited to us over there! If we care not for ourselves in honor, for others in love; if we toil not to-day for the rest "to-morrow," why should He or others this side of Him care for us?

We wish and pray that more of our working-men may have better homes; that they may more earnestly care for their earnings, their lives, their manhood. Those who do not are not the happy ones. Nor are their families. Not care to hoard, but to beautify, to adorn, to clothe, to educate. The noblest men in the land are the sons of working-men, mechanics, laborers, farmers, who have oft been sneered at on account of their poverty. The happiest homes are those built on the enduring foundation of honest toil. We would see every home happy. Would throw open the musty parlors, swing the blinds, clear out the dust and cobwebs; fill closets with clothes, libraries with books, cupboards with food, the home with laughter and cheerfulness, and the heart with joy. We would see the wife and little ones happier, the husband more contented and encouraged, parents more proud of and kind to their children, children set good examples and taught good manners, with neatness and gentleness.

And we would see men of hearts and desires to do good, stand closer by each other and by the unfortunate, to protect and love.

We would ignore and abolish the laws which now rob the working-man of hard-earned money for the benefit of those who pay no taxes on ill-gotten incomes; would wipe out as with red-hot fire the prohibition which comes to us through Puritanism, and lay the foundation for high deeds, noble resolves, great undertakings, and that success which marks our progression to worthiness of future greatness by the firesides and in the homes of the working-men of the land, who are our real and only princes for the present, and joint heirs for the future.

Who of our friends — of our readers — of the public we strive, but can do so little for — will have the pluck to begin a new life and devote more time and more of his earnings to making his home more attractive than perchance it may be this Saturday Night.

XXVII.

The Old Woman.

THIS Saturday Night, as we were walking home chatting with a little six-year-old girl from whom we had bought a little bouquet, we saw a great burly man run against a fruit-stand and upset it. A few oranges and pineapples rolled into the gutter, while an old, wrinkled, sad-faced woman, with rheumatic joints, tried to fix up the broken stand. To say, "Here, stranger! settle with the good woman," was but natural; but he blustered on, only turning his head to mutter, —

"Hang your old woman; let her keep out of the way!"

Now, this was all very independent, for it showed that he who hastened on was a man! But we felt like hating him from that moment. A great, large man, and so unfeeling! We pity his mother. We pity him, aye, more than we did the old woman whose fruit we helped the little girl pick up, and whose broken fruit-stand we helped fix. He needs pity, as any man does who has a brutal heart. And we pity his mother, who would never have thought this of her boy.

Only an old woman!

We do not like any person who does not show love and respect for the aged ones, who at best can be with us but a little while. God knows, the sorrows that come naturally about the sundown of life as swallows homeward fly, are more than we know of, and he is unworthy the name of man who is not kind to the aged. No matter if they are at times cross and peevish. The spar which lies a wreck on the beach, listening to the roar and whisperings of the ocean it once rode upon, has reason to be warped and rough! So with those who have battled in vain with life and grown heart-weary over its trials, sorrows, and disappointments.

Who was this old woman?

We know not. And from her sad face we judge none others know! *But Once?* Yes, once she was a baby,—sweet, smiling, winsome. Then she was petted and admired. The years came in turns and laid their wreaths at her feet, and on them she stepped to womanhood. Then her eyes were bright, her step elastic, and her young heart was filled with the gentle whispers of that love which so often leads to but seldom occupies the charming castles of its wondrous creating. Then she was not old nor ugly. Smiles like bits of golden sunshine pictured her face as lovers gazed thereon. Her hand was not skinny as now when it rested in his years ago, nor was her eye filled with ashes of life and love as now.

Then she was not an old woman, but was fair and sweet, perchance like the one the brusque, brutal man was going to visit to-night; the one he too will abuse if the years rest shadows on her face and form till she becomes an old woman. The man who is not good to the old will be cruel and spiteful to any one he may profess to love when the fantasies of desire have feasted their fill; and there comes even a momentary despondency to the best of hearts.

They were years of the past when she was young.. Then some "old woman" was caring for the man who has no little heart for the aged. And she who is now old had her loves, her hopes, her dreamings of the future. The love-light came to and went from her eye, as words from the heart of another called beautiful visions to her future beholding. The cares of life came to her. One by one troubles settled round her path like beasts of prey waiting to spring on innocent victims. The hopes of early years went one by one out, filled or unfilled, but never more to return, for the links of life have no second coming.

Companions of younger days went to their new homes here or in the hereafter, leaving the woman who is now old. The hours of sickness, the grave; thus, one by one, went her sunshines to shades, and for each loss or hope unfilled came a wrinkle, as time kept most faithful account! God pity her now, for her charms sleep under the sod of the terrible past, never more to come to grace her face or form till the renewal of all this in the beautiful home over the river.

The young live in the future; none of us, or

very few, live in the present; the old live in the past, and their sunset hours are more upon fading than growing pictures. And while the young array and look at the ribbons for the morrow, the old must content be with resting eyes on the weeds of the past, and their hearts on deeds of goodness or charity. How few of us think of the old people! Cares of business or hopes for pleasure drive them from our hearts. Perhaps it was so with them once, yet we hope it will not be so with us. It is up hill to the summit, or down to the grave, and the path down the mountain is slower than the one going up!

We pity the aged. Looking on their faded beauty, their weakening steps, their decrepit forms, we often wonder what we shall do when thus we come to their milestones, if, so be it, ours be the travel so far before comes the nearing shore. If the years come, the joys of now must go! It will not be always that we can be strong and earnest, filled with hot blood, deep desires, and an appetite for the varied dishes of life, from which we, who are in the full flush of health and vigor of maturing years, enjoy.

The touch of love which now sends that wild, delirious thrill from soul to soul will in time be less than now. The flowers will become tangled vines laden with memories, but devoid of that beauty now so charming. The prizes for which we all grasp will come and go, and we will be kindly dealt by in God's own good way as we have been kind to the poor and the aged ones here with us, but not long to stay. Do not pass them roughly by. What was once all theirs, is now all ours; or it will be soon. And what is ours will some day belong to others! Life, nor riches, nor greatness rests with us alone forever. We drink and pass the cup! The train darts by: others saw it before; they will after we have gazed thereon.

It costs but little to be kind to the aged. And kind words fall on old hearts like dew on fading flowers, bringing anew the fragrance of the past. Be kind to the aged people, who toil and strive, that they may not be burdensome. Not alone to those who gave you bone and blood, but to all. It is wicked to be cruel to departing guests, who so soon are going to more beautiful homes than ours here on earth, where all are alike loved, and where all find the rest which we hope will be when shall come to us the final Saturday Night.

XXVIII.

The Family Record.

SATURDAY NIGHT again! How the weeks come and go, singly here; blended into one varied past as they are called to His presence. To-night we opened the Bible by chance, at the Family Record. Singular! Exactly between the old and the new; the past and the coming, so far as effects our future.

Born!

Married!

Died!

Three words, and the sum of life is told.

Born — and who cares for us? Only one or two.

Married — and who cares for us? As if there were more than one to answer!

Died — O God! let us not be forgotten by those who say they love us, and who will not forget us, no matter whether married or died, given or mated, here or hence. Little would there be of life did not some one love us; did we not think that some heart would hold our memory sacred, that 'way over the wondrous river, where the skies are brighter, the seasons more even, the joys sweeter, would we find waiting us, or stand waiting the coming of the loved.

At best it is but a short stay here. Hardly long enough to become acquainted. Merely an evening call, and — good-by! But so it is written, and so we are content. No one escapes death. We do not wish to. It makes but little difference whether we go at noon or sundown, if our new home be happy. Without a doubt or tremble we are ready to go, for ours is that full faith which has long since made the heart entirely at rest concerning the future. When the carriage comes we are ready to go; meanwhile, we will look at the pictures, chat with our friends, or put the house a little more in order for those who remain, that they may not be compelled to do the work we might have done.

And yet we do not care to go. All these beautiful skies, bright stars, trees, hills, rivulets, lakes, flowers, and the pastimes for humanity, will remain for others as toilet articles are left after we have gone to the party. We can part from the beauty of this world, for the flowers are over yonder. Buds here, flowers there. And we shall not care for the beauties we leave when at rest over there! Age puts away the toys of childhood, for they are no longer wanted.

But we had rather stay than go, for we do not know who will care for our loved ones! Who will look over all the little scrolls of paper, —the letters, memorandums, and keepsakes? Somebody. And they will smile at our odd fancies, and wonder why this little thing be here, and that one there, saved so carefully.

Little will they know the history each could tell, or why we prized them to preserve. Never breeze more laden with odor of perfume than these little keepsakes are with memories. Why we walk back to the distant bank of the past on these stepping-stones in the stream, others cannot see!

And who will care for the ones we love? Who will care for her who gave us that priceless jewel years ago? Who will care for the one who for years has been so good, so pure, so true, so kind, so loving? This is the only real sting death has. They who walk hand in hand, palm in palm, for years on the road, cannot bear to part. Who will care for the one who with us, years ago, stepped, as it were, behind the screen, to weld hearts for the future? For this we would live; for, the longer together on earth, the less time to wait for each other in heaven, as the beautiful home we are going to is called.

Who will protect her? Who will hold her to his heart, and open so wide the doors thereto that she may enter and know that all within is hers? Who will love her as we do? Who will hold her hand, still her troubles, look so truly and tenderly in her eyes, as we feel to? Who will bear with her nervous hours, her little forgettings, her sad moments, her need of love, as we would? In all this great big world God gave us is not one we would give her to. They may take our houses and lands, our books, pictures, letters, keepsakes, jewels, life, reputation, take all, for they are but things of our creation, prized more in the chase than capture; but God gave *us* to each other, and may we be not long parted. She has been so good to us, so kind, so true, so earnest. Never a wrong has she done us, or falsehood told. When came the storm, to our heart she came for shelter. When there was beauty in the sky, 'twas she who pointed it out to us.

When others said we would fail, 'twas she who said we could not and would not, for love would sustain us. To be sure, ours was but the home of a working-man, but never did walls contain more priceless treasure. When others were cold and cruel in words, she was good and kind. When others doubted our purpose or honor, she never did, and thus made us strong and invincible.

And her hand has soothed our pain, stilled the

temples wildly throbbing; her eye gone into the depths of that darkness which, like a fog of Hades, at times envelops the stoutest and brightest heart, to drive it away; her kiss has brought life and warmth to energies; her words have so often kindled anew the fires of hope on an ash-covered hearth; her life, ideas, wishes, hopes, future and eternal resting have so woven in with ours that the great joy of life brings the great sting of death!

Who will protect the one we so love *then?* It is the only agony approaching dissolution doth bring. Will she be tempted? Perhaps, for all are. Will she fall? No, a million times *no!* Will she suffer? No, for we will work and save lest the one or ones so dear to us should come to want. No, we must not let her suffer; we will guard against that, and if she be good and not selfish, this care will make her love us the more. And herein confess we to tenfold selfishness! But we cannot help it.

.And so we work, and love, and labor, and look to the future that we may not leave her, the best loved of all, to suffer, to mourn when we are sleeping undisturbed, visited only by her; she may be cared for, wrapped and safe in the mantle woven by our hands while on earth. We will earn a home. Will not lose it in dissipation. Will not tarnish our love for her by contact with all; will not spoil the beautiful dinner she is ever preparing for us alone, by partaking of here a little and there a little as homeward we journey. He who truly loves knows what this means, and it means more than it contains words.

The winds might blow very, very cold on her, and who would wrap the mantle of true love about her; for who would know her worth as do we? And we know her heart would go down like lead into the waters of bitterness when came the hour which said, "No more can he come." Others might be good to her, and kind, and gentle. But what is their "good" to our love, their "kind" to our adoration, their "gentle" to our worship? And there are others who would mourn as we would, should they go down before us, but these could live and love, comforted in their loves, which would absorb grief even for the dearest friends.

And we should feel so sad and heartsore to think we must die or go home without having all the unkind words we may have hastily spoken, forgiven. Oh, how the memory of unkind words lives in the heart! Let us not speak them to the ones we love. Let us be better, more kind and gentle, bearing with each other, for none are quite perfect, none except our loves. And if they are, we must not speak unkindly; if they are not, we must forgive them! Our homes may not be palaces; we may be children of toil; but we can have palaces in our hearts, and live happier than we do if we but strive aright, for he who wins by earnest striving best knows and enjoys the reward.

We will strive, if we are poor. We will be a man, no matter how soon we may go or how long we may stay. We will do by her as we promised in the years of the past, when, speaking by the card of ordainment, each soul said, "I have found it!" And as we thus care for her will she love us, and we will save our own respect. And thus we can do good, can be of use, can more enjoy the beauty of life, and when our name is placed on the family record as *Died*, shall know we live in memory and are thought of oftener than every Saturday Night.

XXIX.

The Poor Old Man.

WE buried him this afternoon at four o'clock.

Just out of the city, in a corner of the graveyard, where the weeds, more tender than flowers, grow rank and close over the poor. Lats Saturday Night we saw him on the street, slowly walking to a cheap home. Seventy-eight years old, and no home of his own; not a child or a chick to give him welcome night, but all waiting to bid him "good morning" over yonder on the flower-lined bank.

He never begged. A sad, strange look was always upon him. Yet he was not cross nor ugly. He was cheerful, and would sit for hours talking to little children, and watching them at play. At times a few tears would fall from his eyes, to be wiped from his furrowed cheek on the back of his wrinkled hand. He lived in a little house back on the prairie; a half-hovel affair; and no one lived with him. Sundays the children would visit him, and bring water from a distant well, and wood by the armful. He gave them nothing but kind words, but they brought him bread, and meat, and fruit, and papers from our sanctum; and when he was too lame to go out, the boys and girls would wait on him. Sometimes he would sit by the hour telling stories to his little friends. He told the boys how to make arrows, and kites, and cross-guns.

And he told them how to cure their sore toes and sore fingers, and when to fish; and that it was wrong to be ugly and cross.

Tuesday evening one of the boys came and wanted us to go to Uncle Benny's cabin, for he was sick. We found him on his cot, very low and feeble. A cruel fever was warring upon that old body. Then we went for a physician, and with the old man staid till morning, when others came. His little friends brought oranges and lemons, jellies and wines from their homes. And a clean sheet was put under him, another over him; cooling drinks were given him, anxious faces were all about him; but Friday morning, just as the sun rose above the bluff east of the city, his head slowly fell back, his mouth opened, there was a rattle in his throat, and as the sunshine struck the little cabin his soul went out, riding on the golden beams of a new life.

Gently we gave him to the winding-sheet, and more carefully combed than usual was the straggling hair which wanted to creep down over his forehead, to see if the eyes were never more to open! And a few kind women made him a shroud, slighting never a part thereof. And a few men bought a neat coffin, paid the sexton, and this afternoon, men and women, and boys and girls, slowly walked behind him to his rest. We have attended burials, but never saw more tear-filled eyes than when the little ones looked for the last time upon poor Uncle Benny, as the coffin-lid was opened just before he was lowered to the great rest. No one knew him other than as Uncle Benny, though for years he had come and gone with his crutch. His face was noble yet sad in its death-look, but it was not of suffering.

And we went with others back to the silent

cabin. How more than lonely it seemed! Two chairs taken from a neighbor's house on which to rest the coffin. A quaint old arm-chair, with a piece of worn sheepskin for cushion; a little old stove, a few tin dishes; an old box serving purpose of table and chest; a few old garments in pieces, some liniment in a bottle, and a few little articles worth nothing.

"What shall we do with them?"

"Oh, you take them; look. them over and do as you please, said they."

In one corner of the chest was an old Bible, badly torn. And a little box, very, very old, as if made by a boy years ago. It would hold a quart, perhaps. It was tied seven times around with a peice of stout cord like a chalk-line. In it were a pair of dingy silk gloves, once white, but now faded into a sickly yellow. They were much too small for his hands. And a very old needle or pin cushion of black cloth, the size of an apple. And a letter, old, dingy, greased, and creased, folded in a piece of soft leather. And a plain gold ring, not much broader than the line of life in our palm.

The letter was too old to read. Its age no one could tell. But in it, on a peice of thick paper, in ink, long since bleached into faintest lines we read, —

"Married — In Albany, May 6, 1813, Benjamin Waldower to Elizabeth Van Dorn."

And this was all. But it told its own story. Then we turned the paper over, to read written on the back of it, the lines, almost indistinct, —

"Died — In Newburg, February 17, 1814, Elizabeth Waldower and infant son."

The story of a life! Poor old man! And this was his treasure; that was the ring. Oh, how long the years must have seemed while he was waiting to go to his loved ones! And have they grown old there as he did here? Will he find them as they went, or have they felt years added where there are no years?

But will it not be grand when we can, at appointed time, solve the wondrous mystery, and know that of which we now know nothing? When we shall have pierced the veil, and gone home to rest with the loved ones there waiting?

Who would fear to die or dread death? Surely not those who have so long been true to and waited for the rejoining the loved ones. If he had only told us his history!

All over the land are poor old men, who have loved as we love, who have been young—have, with beating hearts, held heads upon bosoms, and lingered to revel in the perfume of kisses taken from lips, perhaps, long since gone, as we must all go! The old men were once young. They loved, and longed for twilight hours, as do those who now watch and wait the expected coming; and the years crept slowly upon them, leaving line upon line, care upon care, joy upon joy, but more sorrows upon sorrows. But is it not terrible—this waiting to join those you love?

Waiting the coming of the dear ones of the heart. Hours — days — weeks — months — years come and go while the weary, hungry soul, ever reaching for something not given it here on earth, doubts, fears, then hopes in the fullest of faith concerning the meeting and rejoicing in the eternal land, where there will be no more unfilled desires, for they rest forever in the grave.

Let us all be good and kind to the poor old men; God only knows what they have suffered, or when their hopes were buried. We are all growing old, are all going home; and it may be those we despise on earth will be our guides and patterns in the future. Be kind to the aged. A few more Saturday Nights is all they will be with us, even if their presence should bother and annoy those who are utterly selfish. God only knows how much they sorrow and suffer. Let us make them happy. Let us be kind to each other. Uncle Benny was poor — a poor old man; but he died rich. We all paid tearful tribute to his memory. He was good. He was kind. He was deserving. He was not a miserly, selfish, sordid old man, as are many who live and die, leaving not one sincere mourner. And as we grow old, may we all be like him in having a place in the hearts of those who follow them in proper time! We'd rather sleep beside him in that quiet corner, than under the marble monument of a cold, selfish man; for he would be better company in the city of the dead and of the hereafter, where there is a happy reunion for all who love here on earth; where the day is eternal, and there is no weary Saturday Night.

XXX.

The Old Bureau Drawers.

LAST Saturday Night she was playing about the house, her merry laugh and childish prattle having more of sunshine for those who loved her than ever fell at once on widest forest or prairie. We all loved her. She was winning; and never was a dearer little darling. One night she romped a little too much. Her nerves, not strong, like her mother's or her father's, were overwrought in play; she became fretful, as we all do, and her papa spoke harshly. Then the tears came to her Heaven-lit eyes, and she ran to rest her tired brain in the lap of her mamma.

We heard the cross words; a leaden door seemed to close on our heart as we looked at the innocent prattler, then at the stern man, who was kind, but who forgot himself, and forgot that tender plants crush easily. Over the household came a shadow. The child's voice rang out no more in merriment; we all felt sort of sad, dark, trembly, like as if we wanted to say something, but could not.

And the next day our little friend was sick. The doctor came. She had over-played, taken cold, and suffered. The next day she grew worse. More than one prayer went up to Him from her father; but one from the mother, for her's was all prayer. The next day she was worse, and the next day, resting her head on the bosom of her mother, she sank to sleep. The little curl before us, in a little box, is all there is left to us, a friend of the family, of the little darling. We did not know how well we loved her till she went home to commence another term!

. . . .

This Saturday Night we called in to say a word to those who have loved and lost. The merry laugh, the childish voice, the romping over the floor, the climbing into our lap, the efforts to tease, and the scamperings here and there were all gone. Great tears had spread themselves over the mother's eyes, the voice of the father was low and hushed, for the dearest darling of all was away. God knows we pitied them. We pitied him, for he would have given his own life to have recalled the sharp words. But she had gone home with them, a scar upon her heart, tender and painful.

We sat and talked, and, manly or not, our tears came with theirs, to drop into the cloud of sorrow before us. And while he sat, with hands on table, and head resting thereon, trying to reach to her for the words he had given, and the life he had lost, we went with her into another room. She carried a lamp. It was a poor man's house, and not fitted with gas and conveniences, as are the houses of the rich. Steadily the door was opened. The two windows were darkened by curtains. In a corner of the room stood an old bureau. She pulled out a drawer, next but one to the top, and there were piled and packed all the little clothes of the one we mourned.

The little dresses were there. The little shoes and stockings were in one corner, while in another were the little toys, once the delight of our little pet. There were little ribbons, such teeny little ones. And little cups and saucers, as she had played with them. But *she* was not there. The little clothes she wore a week since were all there, folded nicely, as were the beautiful little hands we saw in the coffin, folded over her breast, as if she was saying, —

"Now I lay me down to sleep."

And the little apron she had torn by catching it as she ran past a wood box, and for which came the cutting words. This too lay there, folded with the rest, just as she had worn it and torn it. In a little box were one, two, three, four little curls, golden and beautiful, and one of them for us. You who are rich do not always know which are the rarest treasures!

The tears of the mother dropped fast into the second grave of her lost one. Never a word did either speak; her heart was, oh! so far away. ' And as the drawer was closed, and silently we returned to another room with our treasure, we could not help thinking of others who mourn for little ones, of the thousands of drawers or little boxes all over the land wherein are kept most sacredly the tear-wet mementoes of the loved ones who have gone before. Dearer than life are these treasures. Here mothers can weep and pray; here the heart can overflow its bitterness, and take another look, and leap toward the beautiful future, where are waiting those we loved, but who have gone.

And as you would meet there the dear ones of the heart, speak kindly. Another Saturday Night, and you may be childless. Another Saturday Night, and your tears may drop in upon the little folded clothes and playthings. And it must be hard to know that our lost ones carried with them hearts covered with the bruises our lips or acts have made. God, who is good, grant that none who read this may have these lasting graves with them now, or with them when shall come another Saturday Night, for we would have no heart filled with sadness. And not for the result of a life of toil would we have our little darling die; perhaps her last thought be of words to her spoken which cut and wounded. You see we cannot call back the words, nor our lost ones, to ask them to forgive us.

All the evening we have sat and thought of the bureau drawers which hold more than the clothes of the little darling who died,— they hold the hearts of the living. They are rounds in the ladder which reaches 'way up there beyond the blue and into the golden; beyond the clouds into the smiles. In palaces and fine mansions, where hired nurses care for little ones, these drawers are not so richly freighted; but in the homes of the poor, yes, and in some of the homes of the rich, they hold more than tongue can tell.

Then let us love our little ones more. Let us always speak kindly to them. Then they will love us and try to do right. And if we go home to rest in the beautiful land before they go, they will love our memories and so live as to meet us. As yet we have no bureau drawer over which to weep. God grant we never may have. But we often think of those who have, and wonder if those who mourn were kind to the little ones whose mounds are in the churchyards, but whose playthings are folded and put away, as is our work for this Saturday Night.

SATURDAY NIGHT IMPROMPTU TO MY DARLING.

DARLING! before to-night I close my eyes
   In sleep, an earnest kiss to thee I send
By the loved spirits. A sweet surprise
And welcome as the glances from thine eyes
   When on thy lips mine did oft attend —
A pure, lingering kiss of love,
                Darling, good-night!

Saturday Night! would that I were by thy side,
   Palm on palm resting as in hours of yore;
When to my kisses you with like replied,
And our hearts in love grew strong allied,
   Waiting love's rest on the eternal shore.
Interest on those kisses now I send,
                Darling, good-night!

Heart loved, I pray "Our Father" each night to bless
   The one to whom I send this kiss of love;
And then I linger on the last caress
You gave me, and, Darling, I must confess
   I think more of it than of Him Above!
Then take this kiss for thee alone —
                Darling, good-night!

THE END.

NEW BOOKS

And New Editions Recently Issued by CARLETON, Publisher, New York,

[Madison Square, corner Fifth Av. and Broadway.]

N. B.—THE PUBLISHERS, upon receipt of the price in advance, will send any of the following Books by mail, POSTAGE FREE, to any part of the United States. This convenient and very safe mode may be adopted when the neighboring Booksellers are not supplied with the desired work. State name and address in full.

Marion Harland's Works.

ALONE.—	A novel.	12mo. cloth,	$1.50
HIDDEN PATH.—	do.	do.	$1.50
MOSS SIDE.—	do.	do.	$1.50
NEMESIS.—	do.	do.	$1.50
MIRIAM.—	do.	do.	$1.50
THE EMPTY HEART.—	do.	do.	$1.50
HELEN GARDNER'S WEDDING-DAY.—		do.	$1.50
SUNNYBANK.—	do.	do.	$1.50
HUSBANDS AND HOMES.—	do.	do.	$1.50
RUBY'S HUSBAND.—	do.	do.	$1.50
PHEMIE'S TEMPTATION.—*Just Published.*		do.	$1.50

Miss Muloch.

JOHN HALIFAX.—A novel. With illustration. 12mo. cloth, $1.75
A LIFE FOR A LIFE.— . do. do. $1.75

Charlotte Bronte (Currer Bell).

JANE EYRE.—A novel. With illustration. 12mo. cloth, $1.75
THE PROFESSOR.— do. . do. . do. $1.75
SHIRLEY.— . do. . do. . do. $1.75
VILLETTE.— . do. . do. . do. $1.75

Hand-Books of Society.

THE HABITS OF GOOD SOCIETY; thoughts, hints, and anecdotes, concerning nice points of taste, good manners, and the art of making oneself agreeable. . . 12mo. cloth, $1.75

THE ART OF CONVERSATION.—A sensible and instructive work, that ought to be in the hands of every one who wishes to be either an agreeable talker or listener. 12mo. cloth, $1.50

ARTS OF WRITING, READING, AND SPEAKING.—An excellent book for self-instruction and improvement. 12mo. cloth, $1.50

HAND-BOOKS OF SOCIETY.—The above three choice volumes bound in extra style, full gilt ornamental back, uniform in appearance, and in a handsome box. . . . $5.00

LIST OF BOOKS PUBLISHED

Mrs. Mary J. Holmes' Works.

'LENA RIVERS.—	A novel.	12mo. cloth,	$1.50
DARKNESS AND DAYLIGHT.—	do.	do.	$1.50
TEMPEST AND SUNSHINE.—	do.	do.	$1.50
MARIAN GREY.—	do.	do.	$1.50
MEADOW BROOK.—	do.	do.	$1.50
ENGLISH ORPHANS.—	do.	do.	$1.50
DORA DEANE.—	do.	do.	$1.50
COUSIN MAUDE.—	do.	do.	$1.50
HOMESTEAD ON THE HILLSIDE.—	do.	do.	$1.50
HUGH WORTHINGTON.—	do.	do.	$1.50
THE CAMERON PRIDE.—	do.	do.	$1.50
ROSE MATHER.—	do.	do.	$1.50
ETHELYN'S MISTAKE.—*Just Published.*	do.	do.	$1.50

Miss Augusta J. Evans.

BEULAH.—A novel of great power.		12mo. cloth,	$1.75
MACARIA.— do. do.		do.	$1.75
ST. ELMO.— do. do.		do.	$2.00
VASHTI.— do. do. *Just Published.*	do.		$2.00

Victor Hugo.

LES MISÉRABLES.—The celebrated novel. One large 8vo volume, paper covers, $2.00 ; . . . cloth bound, $2.50
LES MISÉRABLES.—Spanish. Two vols., paper, $4.00 ; cl., $5.00
JARGAL.—A new novel. Illustrated. 12mo. cloth, $1.75
CLAUDE GUEUX, and Last Day of Condemned Man. do. $1.50

Algernon Charles Swinburne.

LAUS VENERIS, AND OTHER POEMS.— . 12mo. cloth, $1.75

Captain Mayne Reid's Works—Illustrated.

THE SCALP HUNTERS.—	A romance.	12mo. cloth,	$1.75
THE RIFLE RANGERS.—	do.	do.	$1.75
THE TIGER HUNTER.—	do.	do.	$1.75
OSCEOLA, THE SEMINOLE.—	do.	do.	$1.75
THE WAR TRAIL.—	do.	do.	$1.75
THE HUNTER'S FEAST.—	do.	do.	$1.75
RANGERS AND REGULATORS.—	do.	do.	$1.75
THE WHITE CHIEF.—	do.	do.	$1.75
THE QUADROON.—	do.	do.	$1.75
THE WILD HUNTRESS.—	do.	do.	$1.75
THE WOOD RANGERS.—	do.	do.	$1.75
WILD LIFE.—	do.	do.	$1.75
THE MAROON.—	do.	do.	$1.75
LOST LEONORE.—	do.	do.	$1.75
THE HEADLESS HORSEMAN.—	do.	do.	$1.75
THE WHITE GAUNTLET.—*Just Published.*		do.	$1.75

A. S. Roe's Works.

A LONG LOOK AHEAD.—	A novel.	12mo. cloth,	$1.50
TO LOVE AND TO BE LOVED.—	do. . .	do.	$1.50
TIME AND TIDE.—	do. . .	do.	$1.50
I'VE BEEN THINKING. —	do. . .	do.	$1.50
THE STAR AND THE CLOUD.-	do. . .	do.	$1.50
TRUE TO THE LAST.—	do. . .	do.	$1.50
HOW COULD HE HELP IT?—	do. . .	do.	$1.50
LIKE AND UNLIKE.—	do. . .	do.	$1.50
LOOKING AROUND.—	do. . .	do.,	$1.50
WOMAN OUR ANGEL.—	do. . .	do.	$1.50
THE CLOUD ON THE HEART.—	.	do.	$1.50

Orpheus C. Kerr.

THE ORPHEUS C. KERR PAPERS.—Three vols.		12mo. cloth,	$1.50.
SMOKED GLASS.—New comic book. Illustrated.		do.	$1.50
AVERY GLIBUN.—A powerful new novel.—		8vo. cloth,	$2.00

Richard B. Kimball.

WAS HE SUCCESSFUL?—	A novel.	12mo. cloth,	$1.75
UNDERCURRENTS.—	do. . .	do.	$1.75
SAINT LEGER.—	do. . .	do.	$1.75
ROMANCE OF STUDENT LIFE.—do.	. .	do.	$1.75
IN THE TROPICS.—	do. . .	do.	$1.75
HENRY POWERS, Banker.—*Just Published.*		do.	$1.75

Comic Books—Illustrated.

ARTEMUS WARD, His Book.—Letters, etc.		12mo. cl.,	$1.50
DO.	His Travels—Mormons, etc.	do.	$1.50
DO.	In London.—Punch Letters.	do.	$1.50
DO.	His Panorama and Lecture.	do.	$1.50
JOSH BILLINGS ON ICE, and other things.—		do.	$1.50
DO.	His Book of Proverbs, etc.	do.	$1.50
WIDOW SPRIGGINS.—By author " Widow Bedott."		do.	$1.75
FOLLY AS IT FLIES.—By Fanny Fern.	.	. do.	$1.50
CORRY O'LANUS.—His views and opinions.		. do.	$1.50
VERDANT GREEN.—A racy English college story.		do.	$1.50
CONDENSED NOVELS, ETC.—By F. Bret Harte.		do.	$1.50
THE SQUIBOB PAPERS.—By John Phœnix.		. do.	$1.50
MILES O'REILLY.—His Book of Adventures.		. do.	$1.50
DO.	Baked Meats, etc.	. do.	$1.75

"Brick" Pomeroy.

SENSE.—An illustrated vol. of fireside musings.		12mo. cl.,	$1.50
NONSENSE.— do. do. comic sketches.		do.	$1.50

Joseph Rodman Drake.

THE CULPRIT FAY.—A faery poem. .		. 12mo. cloth,	$1.25
THE CULPRIT FAY.—An illustrated edition. 100 exquisite illustrations. . . 4to., beautifully printed and bound.			$5.00

Children's Books—Illustrated.

THE ART OF AMUSING.—With 150 illustrations.	12mo. cl.,	$1.50
FRIENDLY COUNSEL FOR GIRLS.—A charming book.	do.	$1.50
THE CHRISTMAS FONT.—By Mary J. Holmes.	do.	$1.00
ROBINSON CRUSOE.—A Complete edition.	do.	$1.50
LOUIE'S LAST TERM.—By author "Rutledge."	do.	$1.75
ROUNDHEARTS, and other stories.— do.	do.	$1.75
PASTIMES WITH MY LITTLE FRIENDS.—	do.	$1.50
WILL-O'-THE-WISP.—From the German.	do.	$1.50

M. Michelet's Remarkable Works.

LOVE (L'AMOUR).—Translated from the French.	12mo. cl.,	$1.50
WOMAN (LA FEMME).— . do. . .	do.	$1.50

Ernest Renan.

THE LIFE OF JESUS.—Translated from the French.	12mo.cl.,	$1.75
THE APOSTLES.— . . do. . .	do.	$1.75

Popular Italian Novels.

DOCTOR ANTONIO.—A love story. By Ruffini.	12mo. cl.,	$1.75
BEATRICE CENCI.—By Guerrazzi, with portrait.	do.	$1.75

Rev. John Cumming, D.D., of London.

THE GREAT TRIBULATION.—Two series.	12mo. cloth,	$1.50
THE GREAT PREPARATION.— do.	do.	$1.50
THE GREAT CONSUMMATION. do.	do.	$1.50
THE LAST WARNING CRY.—	do.	$1.50

Mrs. Ritchie (Anna Cora Mowatt).

FAIRY FINGERS.—A capital new novel.	12mo. cloth,	$1.75
THE MUTE SINGER.— do.	do.	$1.75
THE CLERGYMAN'S WIFE—and other stories.	do.	$1.75

Mother Goose for Grown Folks.

HUMOROUS RHYMES for grown people.	12mo. cloth,	1.25

T. S. Arthur's New Works.

LIGHT ON SHADOWED PATHS.—A novel.	12mo. cloth,	$1.50
OUT IN THE WORLD.— . do. . .	do.	$1.50
NOTHING BUT MONEY.— . do. . .	do.	$1.50
WHAT CAME AFTERWARDS.— do. . .	do.	$1.50
OUR NEIGHBORS.— . do. . .	do.	$1.50

Geo. W. Carleton.

OUR ARTIST IN CUBA.—With 50 comic illustrations.	$1.50
OUR ARTIST IN PERU.— do. do.	$1.50
OUR ARTIST IN AFRICA.—(*In press*) do.	$1.50

John Esten Cooke.

FAIRFAX.—A Virginian novel.	12mo. cloth,	$1.75
HILT TO HILT.— A Virginian novel.	do.	$1.50

www.ingramcontent.com/pod-product-compliance
Lightning Source LLC
Chambersburg PA
CBHW031948230426
43672CB00010B/2095